The Training Space Ltd
22 Barnwell Court
Mawsley
NN14 1FG
United Kingdom
www.thetrainingspace.co.uk

Ordering Information:

Quantity sales. Special discounts are available on quantity purchases by corporations, associations, schools and others. For details, contact the publisher at the address above. Orders by trade bookstores and wholesalers.

Please contact:

The Training Space Ltd
Tel: (+44) 01536 410078
Email: enquiries@thetrainingspace.co.uk
Web: www.thetrainingspace.co.uk

Every effort has been made to obtain the necessary permissions with reference to copyright materials, both illustrative and quoted. We apologise for any omissions in this respect and will be pleased to make appropriate acknowledgements in any future editions.

Printed in the UK.

First edition.

ISBN 978-1-907581-19-9

Sue Crowther - Editor

Designed by James Hunter, Lee Akers & Toby Stubbs
www.studiokaioti.com

A book is a
dream that you
hold in your
hand.

Neil Gaiman

Books are
a uniquely
portable
magic.

Stephen King

Acknowledgements

Lashings of 'thank yous' to all the children I have taught across the UK, who reminded me what a unique and precious job teaching is. Each and every one of you has helped to develop my thinking about teaching and learning.

Scoops of gratefulness to Darren Smith and Emma Wilson at Headlands Primary School, whose exuberant enthusiasm has taught me the perfect recipe for school success.

Special drizzles of gratitude, with extra cupfuls of appreciation, to James Hunter, Lee Akers and Toby Stubbs – the patient and inspirational designers of this book. A ladleful of adoration for my talented niece, Freya Considine, who made some of my loosely-doodled illustrations delectable.

An enormous dollop of indebtedness to my editor, the talented Sue Crowther, whose precise and diligent efforts cooked my ramblings into something wholesome and delicious.

Finally, a generous sprinkling of love for Ian Considine – to compensate for the years that I chewed his ear off about this book.

" I spent my life folded between the pages of books. In the absence of human relationships, I formed bonds with paper characters. I lived love and loss through stories threaded in history; I experienced adolescence by association. My world is one interwoven web of words, stringing limb to limb, bone to sinew, thoughts and images all together. I am a being comprised of letters, a character created by sentences, a figment of imagination formed through fiction. **"**

Tahereh Mafi

" The best moments in reading are when you come across something – a thought, a feeling, a way of looking at things – which you had thought special and particular to you. Now, here it is, set down by someone else, a person you have never met, someone even who is long dead. And it is as if a hand has come out and taken yours. **"**

Alan Bennett

" For some of us, books are as important as almost anything else on earth. What a miracle it is that out of these small, flat, rigid squares of paper unfolds world after world after world, worlds that sing to you, comfort and quiet or excite you. Books help us understand who we are and how we are to behave. They show us what community and friendship mean; they show us how to live and die. **"**

Anne Lamott

" To read is to fly: it is to soar to a point of vantage which gives a view over wide terrains of history, human variety, ideas, shared experience and the fruits of many inquiries. **"**

A. C. Grayling

" The way of words, of knowing and loving words, is a way to the essence of things, and to the essence of knowing. **"**

John Dunne

" Outside of a dog, a book is a man's best friend. Inside of a dog, it's too dark to read. **"**

Groucho Marx

Hooked on Books

Transforming the Teaching of Reading

Jane Considine

The **Training** Space
Transforming teaching and learning

About The Author

Jane has been closely involved in revolutionising reading in primary schools since 2000. At the forefront of teacher training, she provides practical solutions to capitalise on opportunities for reading mastery – so that pupils move from learning to read onto reading to learn.

Reading is a complex interplay between engagement, fluidity, meaning and reflection. Jane is renowned for her 'sleeves up, hands on' approach, which means she can often be found in UK classrooms demonstrating excellence in the teaching of reading.

Many schools adopt a *Book Talk* approach and success can be seen in these schools through their vibrant reading curriculums and excellent reading results. Jane sees the gift of reading as a duty of care that every teacher must make the cornerstone of their work. She recently opened a teachers' centre in Northamptonshire, which is free to visit and boasts a collection of excellent examples of texts for primary-aged children to explore.

Jane provides a systems-based solution to improving the teaching of reading. With reading for pleasure being the biggest single predictor of academic success, a powerful and structured approach to teaching with excellence is required. Jane supports teachers around the country to urgently and vitally ensure children are '*hooked on books*'.

Jane Considine

Thank you for your inspiration and challenging my thinking along the way.

- All Saints C of E (VA) Primary School
- Baldersby St. James C of E Primary School
- Blenheim Primary School
- Boothville Primary School
- Bowling Green Primary School
- Briary Primary School
- Caroline Chisholm School
- Castle Academy
- Chacombe C of E Primary School

- Copley Junior School
- Copthorne Primary School
- Cowlersley Primary School
- Dale House School
- Dimple Well Infant School
- Driffield C of E (VC) Infant School
- Earls Barton Infant School
- East Bierley C of E (VC) Primary School
- Eye C of E Primary School

- Fairburn Community Primary School
- Farley Hill Primary School
- Great Doddington Primary School
- Greatworth Primary School
- Hawksworth C of E Primary School
- Haylands Primary School
- Headlands Primary School
- Hightown Junior, Infant & Nursery School
- Hilltop Primary School
- Hipperholme Grammar School
- Irthlingborough Junior School
- Kettering Buccleuch Academy
- King's Cliffe Endowed Primary School
- Kingsley Primary School
- Kingsthorpe Grove Primary School
- Kippax Ash Tree Primary School
- Kirk Smeaton C of E (VC) Primary School
- Long Buckby Junior School
- Lower Meadow Primary Academy
- Lumbertubs Primary School
- Marshlands Primary School
- Martin Frobisher Infant School
- Naseby C of E Primary Academy
- Netherton Junior and Infant School
- Niton Primary School
- Oakham Primary School
- Otley All Saints C of E Primary School
- Our Lady of Walsingham Catholic Primary School, Northants
- Purlwell Infant & Nursery School
- Ranby C of E Primary School
- Richmond House School
- Rivermead Primary School
- Swingate Infant School
- St. Giles Junior School, Warwickshire
- St. Ignatius' Catholic Primary School, Lancashire
- St. John's C of E (VA) Junior & Infant School, Yorkshire
- St. Mary's C of E Primary Academy, Northants
- St. Nicholas Catholic Primary School, Yorkshire
- St. Patrick's Catholic Primary & Nursery School, Northants
- St. Peter's C of E Primary School, Leicestershire
- St. Andrew's C of E Primary School, Northants
- St. Paul's C of E Primary School, Lancashire
- Sunnyside Primary Academy
- Terrington Hall Preparatory School
- The Merton Primary School
- Thorpe Willoughby Community Primary School
- Thorplands Primary School
- Titchmarsh C of E Primary School
- Vernon Terrace Primary School
- Warmington School
- Weston Favell C of E Primary School
- Whiston Worrygoose Junior & Infant School
- Wilby C of E Primary School
- Willow Academy
- Windmill C of E Primary School

Contents

Stories have infinite power: the power to lead us down troublesome tracks, to have us jumping for joy one moment and submerged in sadness the next. Stories can provide pathways, solve problems, bring solace, shake up our thinking and sometimes even challenge or confirm our own ways of living. For many years, the story of teaching reading has been a tragedy: a tale of heroic endeavours blighted by time pressures and curriculum overload.

Are you desperate for clarity on the teaching of reading? Struggling to find time to teach it well? Lacking direction and focus?

Inside this book you will discover a straightforward, deliverable system for the successful teaching of reading for life. It's effective, supportive and fosters the pleasure principle of reading.

One of our most important duties as teachers is to help pupils fall in love with reading – to introduce them to this worthy, lifelong companion and to nurture their fledgling relationships with it. This requires investment. With time and space, words can sink in deep, but teachers and pupils must commit to exploring books properly and in depth.

As we wander through the webs of words in books, our lives tangle together – providing support, encouragement, advice and learning. This symbiotic relationship grows stronger with the ideas revealed. Writing does not end with the author: it is carried forward in the minds of readers. This is the power and beauty of reading. It has a life of its own.

Pupils do not always find reading to be their friend. They need to know it is the greatest friend they could ever wish for – a constant, a hopeful and trusted soulmate, who will never let them down no matter what. Teachers must facilitate these friendships, and support children who drift apart from them, so that they are never left as grown-ups trying to make sense of the world without the power of words.

Book Talk is a coherent system for teaching the multiple layers of what it means to be an effective reader. This book explains, in depth, how pupils' thinking needs to be stretched and shaped up through the *three zones of reading*. The ideas of reading are explored through the FANTASTICs, the understanding of reading through the STYLISTICs and deeper aspects of reading comprehension through the ANALYTICS.

The Three Zones
Of Reading

1 | Ideas | →

2 | Understanding | →

3 | Competencies | →

Why Is Teaching Reading A Moral Duty?

"If teachers had only one job to do, then it should be bestowing the gift of reading. Without reading, a child's world shrinks and begins to narrow. Opportunities are limited, doors begin to close and self-esteem crumbles. Teachers must get it right."

Chapter 1

Summary

☑ There is a strong link between disadvantage and poor reading skills. Unemployed adults, and those in prison, are twice as likely to have weak literacy skills as those in full-time employment.

☑ Phonics teaching is vital for pupils in the early stages of reading development. The current Year 1 phonics test - based on nonsense words - is futile, as it is a missed opportunity to meet real words. This test should be restructured so that pupils read whole sentences with real-life meaning to them. Differentiated entry points would ease the pressures around phonics teaching, freeing up pupils already able enough to meet more challenging comprehension-based tasks.

☑ The 2014 national curriculum is very much geared towards teachers nurturing and developing a 'love of reading' in pupils.

☑ All teachers have a duty to ensure the teaching of reading is comprehensive, vibrant and develops skills for life. In fact, the richness of a young child's vocabulary is a proven indicator of greater life choices and future earning power.

HOOKED ON BOOKS

Why Is Teaching Reading A Moral Duty?

Reading is fundamental in modern society and shapes us as critical thinkers, learners and questioning citizens. Learning to read, and reading to learn, is the foundation for future educational success. As the singular most important academic skill of our age, teachers have an obligation to ensure **every** pupil is a competent reader.

It is no coincidence that UK prisoners struggle with reading. In November 2015, government data revealed that 46% of those entering the prison system had poor literacy skills (no higher than the reading age of an 11-year-old). The report, *OLASS English and Maths Assessments: Participation 2014/15*, was based on the results of 74,300 prisoners assessed on entering prison for short-term sentences from August 2014. It will also come

as no surprise that the majority of the UK's unemployed population is barely literate. The gap in literacy skills, between unemployed and working young people, is wider in the UK than in any other Western nation. The survey, by the *Organisation for Economic Co-operation and Development (OECD)*, looked at the performance of more than 35 million 16 to 29-year-olds in 22 Western nations. Predictably, the NEETs (young people neither employed nor in education or training) were far more likely to have poor literacy skills. Where skills were low, unemployment was high. Of the young adults who scored at Level 1 or 2 (extremely low literacy), 59% were NEETs. This correlation points to the importance of good literacy as a predictor of future employment success.

OECD (2016) Reading performance (PISA)

However, there are other findings by the OECD that make for even more worrying reading:

• **An estimated nine million adults of working age have low basic skills.**

Their poor or very poor literacy and/or numeracy skills puts England close to the bottom of the OECD rankings. Of particular concern is that while standards in other countries are improving, in England they are not. The performance of older age groups is as good – if not better – than the youngest, while in most countries younger cohorts have greater skills than their elders. At every qualification level, low literacy and numeracy skills are more common among young people in England than in most other OECD countries.

• **In England, one-third of those aged 16-19 have low basic skills.**

Once again, this puts England at or near the bottom of all OECD countries. The OECD also suggests the emphasis here on achieving grade C at GCSE is misplaced, as these students still perform less well in basic skills than their equivalents in other OECD countries.

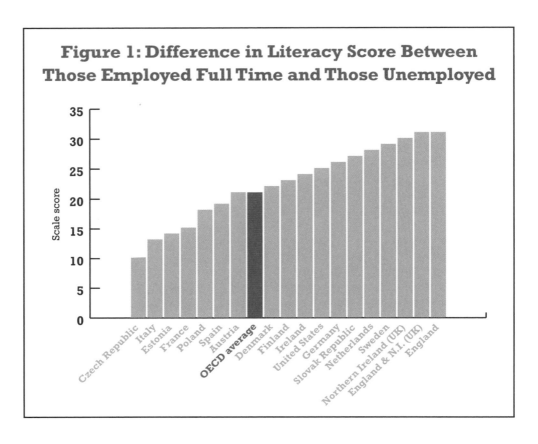

Figure 1: Difference in Literacy Score Between Those Employed Full Time and Those Unemployed

This international picture points to an urgent need to raise the skills of pupils – and reading is a crucial component in the mission to improve literacy standards. It doesn't matter what analogy is used – the flying carpet, the golden key, the magic doorway – reading needs to be taught well, and English primary pupils are less likely to read for pleasure than their counterparts in many other countries. This needs to be addressed quickly and effectively because a thriving reading culture, in a school that values books and promotes high level comprehension strategies, offers pupils the best possible opportunities for life success.

"The inability to read and write effectively diminishes human potential, learning potential, self-esteem, options and choices, the ability to think, make judgements, anticipate implications, think independently, to be adaptable, and the ability to learn and grow throughout life. It leads to personal stress and frustration, family stress, community stress, employment difficulties, diminished workplace options, social difficulties and anti-social behaviours."
Adrienne Nightingale, Reading Recovery Trained Teacher

Reading can be a frustrating business if pupils are not equipped with the correct skills.

Reading must be taught properly, accurately and with a verve that instils excitement and pleasure. It is the most critical part of any teacher's job and must be undertaken with the greatest of care and diligence. In many schools, provision is patchy and standards are too low. As a matter of urgency, those with the responsibility need to shape up a reading curriculum that addresses this underperformance 'head on' and ensures all pupils are readers with an in-depth knowledge of how the written word functions, informs and shapes our understanding of the world around us.

Phonics

Phonics is a critical part of a pupil's reading journey and in the early stages of reading development must be taught in a fun, fast and furious way. This is not a book about phonics. However, it is important to mention its vital role in providing pupils with the most direct route to becoming skilled readers. The *Rose Review (DfES, 2006b)* defined 'high quality systematic phonic work' as teaching novice readers:

- grapheme/phoneme (letter/sound) correspondences (the alphabetic principle) in a clearly defined, incremental sequence;

- the highly important skill of blending (synthesising) phonemes in order, throughout a word, to read it;

- the skill of segmenting words into constituent phonemes to spell;

- that blending and segmenting are reversible processes.

Phonological development – how a child gradually learns to hear, segment and understand small units of sounds – critically affects the child's ability to decode whole words. The more a child is exposed to written words, the greater his or her implicit and explicit understanding of all language. The current national curriculum puts a sharp emphasis on word-reading and outlines in detail the work of Year 1 teachers, which should:

"...build on work from the Early Years Foundation Stage, making sure that pupils can sound and blend unfamiliar printed words quickly and accurately using the phonic knowledge and skills that they have already learned. Teachers should also ensure that pupils continue to learn new grapheme-phoneme correspondences (GPCs) and revise and consolidate those learned earlier. The understanding that the letter(s) on the page represent the sounds in spoken words should underpin pupils' reading and spelling of all words."
National Curriculum in England 2014

In Year 1 classrooms, six year olds are subjected to the high-stakes phonics test. It requires pupils to read made-up words such as *mip, fack, zort, koob* and *glimp*. The fact that these words are nonsensical is the strangest part of this test. If, at the heart of reading, children are to be taught to create meaning, it is a retrograde move by government to test with these types of words – undermining the very nature of reading itself. One of the biggest barriers

Phonics is fundamental. Pupils need to have an understanding of the mechanics of reading.

to pupil achievement is vocabulary – so why not use real words? There are enough real words in the English language with certain phonic patterns, and if these were placed in meaningful sentences, all the better. Currently, in the *Oxford English Dictionary* there are a quarter of a million distinct English words: it is not as if the government would be strapped for choice. Far more useful would have been a test targeting the reading of sentences, with phonically-appropriate words linked to the national curriculum – strengthening pupil understanding of reading for meaning. In my work supporting schools to improve their standards, the phonics curriculum dominates timetables, mainly due to the importance for schools in having healthy phonics data. It seems to

me that many pupils would be ready for the phonics test much earlier in the year, and a more differentiated approach would be beneficial – so that pupils could 'bank' their results and be freed up to explore wider reading strategies.

Reading cannot be all about the mechanics, but the mechanics is essential if the 'magic' is to be discovered. We must ensure pupils are not only proficient decoders but are also lovers of books. Here, author Michael Rosen captures this concern:

"Those children who have already been convinced that reading a whole book will be a great thing to do (probably by their parents reading to them) will have little or no problem

Promoting The Pleasure Principle of Reading

Pupil Book Talk - Conversations about books

Look at Whole Texts - Fewer extracts

Enthusiasm Fostered - Teacher modelled

Active Approaches to Reading

Sustained Reading - Build stamina

Understanding Preferences in Reading

Read Aloud Regularly - Listen to texts read aloud

Experience Range of Texts

Headlands Primary invites parents into school to enjoy the library with their children.

making the leap from phonics to real books and staying with them. For the millions of others who aren't convinced that reading is interesting or cool, no matter how good they are with their phonics, it's not clear why or how they will want to stick with it."

Reading for pleasure is more important for children's cognitive development than their parents' level of education and is a more powerful factor in life achievement than socio-economic background.
OECD (2010) PISA 2009 Results: Learning to Learn – Student Engagement, Strategies and Practices

This finding in the OECD report strengthens the purpose of a teacher's work. It is reinforced in the wording of the national curriculum, which urges teachers to establish 'an appreciation and love of reading' which:

"...feeds pupils' imaginations and opens up a treasure house of wonder and joy for curious young minds."

Schools that foster a strong reading for pleasure ethos promote the following principles:

Pupil Book Talk - Conversations about books

A National Reading Panel review in the United States defined reading as:

'the construction of the meaning of a written text through a reciprocal interchange of ideas between the reader and...a particular text'. **Teaching Children to Read: An Evidence-Based Assessment of the Scientific Research Literature on Reading and its Implications for Reading Instruction.**

This definition hinges on readers finding their own personal interpretations of literary material. Young children need frequent and rich conversations about books to become skilled at both interpretation and the development of robust and authentic personal responses. Great teachers, who facilitate these in-depth discussions around reading, foster pupils' comprehension and analytical skills. Pupils need to glean accurate information from texts, so that they move from the 'gist' mode to a deep and active understanding based on specifics, textual evidence and articulation of their personal views.

Look at Whole Texts -
Fewer extracts

Excerpts, snippets and extracts are reasonable as long as they don't become a pupil's regular diet. Ideally, pupils need to get 'lost in a book', cover to cover, start to finish, because they are reading a great book. Many Key Stage 2 pupils find the leap from the straightforward novel – e.g. *Flat Stanley* (Egmont) or *The Shrinking of Treehorn* (Puffin) – to more challenging texts difficult, but this

shouldn't mean shying away from doing it. Nonetheless, as teachers, this is a time when scaffolding pupils is vital to ensure they embrace the difficulties locked in novels targeted at ages 9-11 and beyond. A whole book carefully crafted over time assists pupils in understanding character development, plot twists and changing themes. The overall portfolio of books that pupils will encounter needs thinking about: for merit, language, cultural commentary, historical interest and/or imparting knowledge. There are many reasons resources need to be rich and varied: the most important of which is inspiring children to read.

It is important pupils read whole novels.

Enthusiasm Fostered
- Teacher modelled

"There are perhaps no days of our childhood we lived so fully as those...we spent with our favourite book. Everything that filled them for others, so it seemed, and that we dismissed as a vulgar obstacle to a divine pleasure: the game for which a friend would come to fetch us at the most interesting passage; the troublesome bee or sun ray that forced us to lift our eyes from the page or to change position; the provisions for the afternoon snack that we had made to take along and that we left beside us on the bench without touching, while above our head the sun was diminishing in force in the blue sky; the dinner we had to return home for, and during which we thought only of going up immediately afterward to finish the interrupted chapter; all those things which reading should have kept us from feeling anything but annoyance, on the contrary they have engraved on us so sweet a memory (so much more precious to our present judgement than what we read then with such love), that if we still happen today to leaf through those books of another time, it is for no other reason than that they are the only calendars we have kept of days that have vanished, and we hope to see reflected on their pages the dwellings and the ponds that no longer exist."

Proust: On Reading

1. How many pupils have found the reading bug?
2. How many pupils have 'sweet memories' of reading?
3. How many pupils choose reading above other activities if given a choice?

Teachers need to hold pupils' hands, open their eyes and navigate their imaginations to delightful worlds waiting to be discovered and explored. Reading enthusiasm can be modelled by teachers and visitors to the school. A school that engages in and celebrates the festivals of *World Book Day* (March), *Children's Book Week* (October) and *National Poetry Day* (Thursday of Children's Book Week) will later be able to trade on the enthusiasm of children who are genuinely excited about books.

Active Approaches to Reading

Reading tasks need to follow lines of enquiry and explore one focus area in depth. This allows pupils to develop answers that are detailed and well supported. Active reading is when pupils are proactively seeking to comment on a line of enquiry and do all they can, in relation to a text, to bring forward a compelling and vigorous case. Pupils need the teacher to model (with another adult in 'devil's advocate' mode) to challenge lines of enquiry – so they can witness first-hand how to argue a point and use counter evidence to strengthen their suggestions and conclusions. The more pupils invest in reading with a 'switched on', excited mind, the more they will benefit and see the gains of working and thinking in this way. Excellent readers are not passive: they engage with the written word in a lively and interactive way. They have the tools to formulate an argument/point of view and challenge other pupils they disagree with, or push their idea

Communicating a love and passion for great books is one of the most important responsibilities of the primary school teacher.

further by adding subsequent information. Strong habits of discussion build resilience in dealing with opposing views and taking on board reasoned arguments from different camps. An active reading classroom is buzzing, drenched in talk and the nature of that talk is complex, intelligent and has direction.

Sustained Reading -
Build stamina

The cognitive scientist, Annie Murphy Paul, in her *Time* article, *Reading Literature Makes Us Smarter and Nicer* explained how during sustained reading (that is frequent and deep) the brain didn't make a distinction between actually experiencing something in real life and reading about it. These readers' brains felt they'd actually encountered 'read about' events. However, 'online' reading didn't build stamina: it had many distractions, was superficial in style and was often based on skimming. Maryanne Wolf argued in her book *Proust and the Squid* that on-screen texts were not read 'inferentially, analytically or critically'. They were 'skimmed and filleted, cherry-picked for half-grasped truths'. Reading a book, she said, was more likely to be a relationship of commitment: longer-lasting, steadier and with proper (if not guilty) time allocated for it.

Understanding Preferences in Reading

What do children like? We know they like computer games, social media and watching clips on *YouTube*. Reading needs certain conditions to be appreciated: a bit of peace and quiet, a comfy spot and the right book! Our communities of children are true digital natives and are often more tech-savvy than the adults trying to teach them. Technology has transformed all of our lives but what if the on-screen reader becomes our only type of reader? What would be lost in the reading brain if we were only transfixed by screens?

The real answer is probably quality: the classification of ideas and information into a larger system of usefulness. The immediacy of the web, and on-screen information, means huge quantities of material are available without critical effort and there is often no sense that we have to go beyond the information provided. Are pupils getting to the heart of the matter when reading on screen? Essentially, the crucial aspect of reading is going beyond the words to find personal meaning. Internet information is quick - practically instant - and there are constant temptations to be lured away from one piece of reading material towards the next hot story.

The right book is actually very hard to find. It can often be a slow process and difficult to ascertain. Even as adults, with a fair idea of what we like, it can still be challenging...

Finding the right book – the struggle is real

1. It looks artistically appealing but the first two pages haven't gripped me.

2. I've read something by this author before; I know I'm going to like it... Oh no! I don't!

3. I like this genre but this is taking a slightly different slant...I'm not sure.

4. I just want to escape...oh dear, not to a war-torn land though.

5. This looks like my cup of tea...ummm, maybe not but my mum would like it.

6. My friend bought it for me. I'll carry it around for at least 4 weeks.

7. It looks so beautiful and makes a lovely coaster.

8. I've spent my whole lunch hour in this bookshop...I can't decide.

9. I just can't find anything that is as good as the last book I read.

10. Aah, I've found the perfect book, but now I don't have time to read it.

Children need help finding their own loves in reading. They often need permission to read cheeky material, such as *Dirty Bertie* by David Roberts and Alan MacDonald (about a boy who can't stop farting) or *I am not a Loser* by Jim Smith (littered with poo, wee and vomit). Some pupils need more

Finding The Right Book

1. It looks artistically appealing but the first two pages haven't gripped me.

2. I've read something by this author before; I know I'm going to like it…Oh no! I don't!

3. I like this genre but this is taking a slightly different slant… I'm not sure.

4. I just want to escape… oh dear, not to a war-torn land though.

5. This looks like my cup of tea…ummm, maybe not but my mum would like it.

6. My friend bought it for me. I'll carry it around for at least 4 weeks.

7. It looks so beautiful and makes a lovely coaster.

8. I've spent my whole lunch hour in this bookshop… I can't decide.

9. I just can't find anything that is as good as the last book I read.

10. Aah, I've found the perfect book, but now I don't have time to read it.

non-fiction material linked to their interests, e.g. *Aston Villa Football Club* or nearly-extinct species. Many children simply need help to achieve their first buzz from a book. If they can fall head over heels in love with an author or the first book in a series, it can often ignite a long and rewarding love affair.

Read Aloud Regularly - Listen to texts read aloud

A story has a different rhythm, tone and intonation to non-fiction and is different again to poetry. Pupils need to let language wash over them so they can hear the differences and begin to connect with writer styles and tones. Steven Pinker eloquently remarked:

"Children are wired for sound, but print is an optional accessory that must be painstakingly bolted on."

Listening to all types of genres read by the teacher, for 10 minutes every day between Foundation Stage and Year 6, is essential in fostering a love of reading. This must be a time in the school day that is relaxed and calm. The teacher doesn't need a learning objective as it will be inextricably tangled up in the process itself. It will not be a time to quiz pupils with probing questions or an opportunity to deconstruct the text for features or language. This reading slot will be a chance for pupils to absorb the words and 'let language wash over them'. In David Liben's research, *Aspects of Text Complexity:*

Vocabulary Research Base, pupils needed a minimum of six repetitions of a word in different contexts before they truly learned it and used it themselves. For this reason alone, pupils need to be exposed to a wealth of words, constructed in a range of ways and for different purposes. Storytime is vital for demonstrating a love and a passion for a wonderful book. It is a chance to inject life into the words and bring what is flat and two-dimensional alive through expression, gesture and rhythm. It connects children with the immediacy of reading and supports their understanding of how to read. Doug Lemov, in *Reading Reconsidered*, captures so poetically the importance of expressive reading to a class. In three words, Doug tells teachers to:

Show Some Spunk

I am unsure of how successfully this American soundbite has transferred to the UK but Lemov qualifies it with the following explanation:

"A particularly important time to Show Some Spunk is at the start of a longer section of oral reading or starting up after a break for discussion. Reading the first few sentences yourself models and normalizes expressiveness and helps engage and sustain interest in the text by getting it off to an exciting start. The verve and energy you bring to oral reading will be reflected in your students' oral (and silent) reading through increased fluency and joy for reading."

Pupils also need practice at reading aloud, especially to their peers, as this helps them improve their articulation. Reading 'like a teacher' also helps them wear a reading personality that might be slightly more confident than their own.

Experience Range of Texts

Schools need to bolster the quality of their non-fiction texts. Key Stage 1 children need access to books about the human body that are bright, colourful and include flaps! Key Stage 2 pupils need more books about the changing body and puberty, as well as information books about emotions, life challenges and issues, e.g. coping with divorce. Non-fiction books serve the purpose of 'killing two birds with one stone'. They improve children's reading skills and also enhance their knowledge of the real world. There always seems to be a shortage in school libraries of quiz books, general knowledge books and the classic *Guinness Book of Records*. All of these texts are intriguing 'ways in' for pupils to plug gaps in their general knowledge and acquire knowledge of different text types and their functions.

Reading helps children to realise their potential and develop empathy. It empowers them to move beyond the words to make informed decisions about their lives. One of the most interesting reports on reading is from the *Institute for Fiscal Studies*. This 2015 longitudinal study of 10 year olds showed the financial benefits of being a good reader:

Reception pupil reading to her friends.

▶ Children with higher reading skills at age 10 see the impact through their salaries more than 25 years later.

▶ A strong reader at age 10 would earn 21% more per hour at age 38, on average, than someone from a similar background with poor reading skills.

Teaching reading is the duty of every primary school teacher and is a task that shouldn't be undertaken lightly. Jim Rose's *Independent Review of the Primary Curriculum* captured the essence of this succinctly in the words of one head teacher:

"If children leave my school and can't paint that's a pity, but if they leave and they can't read that's a disaster."

As we move as a society from a paper-based reading position – to a technological jungle where real and fake information tangle together on the web – we have to reflect more closely on the similarities and differences between books and the online universe. Whilst books are generally honed, polished and well-considered compilations of information, the *Googlesphere* presents us, second by second, with a glut of information (much of which has little educational value). Kindles have somewhat blurred the boundaries but are mainly considered as a book format.

Reading online threatens stamina, as there are many more distractions on the web. Eye movement studies have highlighted greater flickering and 'moving about' of the eyes as they are distracted by 'pop ups', scroll bars and the lure of instant choices available at the touch of a button. These studies have also shown people read websites in an F-shaped pattern. They do not thoroughly read content in a word-for-word manner and the eye is drawn to visuals, subheadings and bullet points. A 2006 study by Jakob Nielsen, *How People Read on the Web*, featured more than 300 participants reading more than 100 web pages. It was noted that their reading style was more 'skimming and scanning' in nature which, as a teacher, suggests to me that reading stamina is definitely on the decline. Readers are increasingly seeking divorce from their committed, gentler relationships with books in exchange for the instant gratification of social media and memes.

Here, author Neil Gaiman and a Year 6 pupil from Northamptonshire explain why

Pupils finding books that they enjoy and having some time to read them.

perseverance with a good book, over a quick fix online, is well worth the investment:

"Fiction has two uses. Firstly, it's a gateway drug to reading. The drive to know what happens next, to want to turn the page, the need to keep going, even if it's hard, because someone's in trouble and you have to know how it's all going to end...that's a very real drive. And it forces you to learn new words, to think new thoughts, to keep going. To discover that reading per se is pleasurable. Once you learn that, you're on the road to reading everything. And reading is key. There were noises made briefly, a few years ago, about the idea that we were living in a post-literate world, in which the ability to make sense out of written words was somehow redundant, but those days are gone: words are more important than they ever were: we navigate the world with words, and as the world slips onto the web, we need to follow, to communicate and to comprehend what we are reading. People who cannot understand each other cannot exchange ideas, cannot communicate, and translation programs only go so far. The simplest way to make sure that we raise literate children is to teach them to read, and to show them that reading is a pleasurable activity. And that means, at its simplest, finding books that they enjoy, giving them access to those books, and letting them read them."
Neil Gaiman

"You must never quit until you get to Chapter 3. As a reader, it's your right not to read if you can't connect with a book but you shouldn't give up too soon. Many authors are lining stuff up in Chapters 1 and 2. Sometimes they are deliberately trying to keep things hidden until they are revealed in Chapter 3. Only when you have given the author a proper chance can you make a decision to walk away."
A Year 6 pupil, working at greater depth in reading and writing, Long Buckby Junior School, Northants

The purpose of this book is to help schools develop a positive and successful reading curriculum. It will offer a wealth of advice and practical guidance on developing a systematic structure for teaching:

i. The pleasure of reading

ii. Comprehension of the written word across a broad spectrum of genres

Reading is fundamental to developing children as thinkers and moving learning forwards. Maryanne Wolf summarises this beautifully:

"the new circuits and pathways that the brain fashions in order to read become the foundation for being able to think in different, innovative ways."

By undertaking this challenge, schools offer wide-reaching benefits to the pupils in their care: higher self-esteem, greater opportunities and a direct impact on their future wellbeing and financial security.

Consider

An audit across Foundation Stage, Key Stage 1 and Key Stage 2. How much time is dedicated to the reading curriculum? In a staff meeting, discuss differences across classes. Separate phonics teaching, as part of the time dedicated to teaching reading, and explore (as a teaching team) the amount and quality of reading experiences.

School Impact Points

Gather internal and external views on the importance and power of reading.

 Collect quotes from pupils, teachers, parents and other key members of your school community. Use the prompts outlined below to get you started:

- I think reading is important because...
- I love reading because...
- We care about reading because...
- Without reading,...
- A good book will...

 Talk to colleagues in a real and honest way about aspects of the job they find challenging and share strategies most likely to have a high impact on standards.

Izzy, Year 4, Age 8

How Do We Give Children The Reading Bug?

"Children need to get the bug. The bug needs to get so bad that it itches in their minds every day. The itch needs to become so overwhelming that they need to scratch it. The only thing that will soothe a reading bug itch is books (and lots of them) because they are good for your health."

Chapter 2

Summary

☑ It is the cumulative effect of many different strategies that shows pupils we care about reading.

☑ Reading needs valuing as a positive homework strategy. Reading done well will bring the most reward and support to pupils in all areas of school life.

☑ Reading culture can be enhanced through clubs, initiatives and teacher action to increase reading opportunities.

☑ Reading environments need to be engaging, so they capture pupils' imaginations, and a library needs to be the 'beating heart' of a school. There are many ways we can enhance pupils' engagement with their school libraries..

HB

How Do We Give Children The Reading Bug?

Not all children enjoy reading. This is a travesty. Children don't have to like all books but we have to help them find the books that do appeal to them. Every child will have books that will have relevance, a truth or be intriguing for their current lives. People who regularly read books are, on average, more satisfied with life, happier, and more likely to feel that the things they do in life are worthwhile. Three-quarters of adults say that reading improves their lives and the same percentage believes it helps to make them feel good. *Jenkins et al (2011) Literacy, Numeracy and Disadvantage Among Older Adults in England.*

This chapter considers how schools can develop a rich reading curriculum and promote a love of reading to all pupils. In the Appendix, you will find a printable resource called 'Every Minute Counts', which highlights the annual word counts from regular daily reading.

Where to start?

Reading must be celebrated in all parts of the school: through the curriculum as well as through the ethos and messages we convey. Books are a great place to start. Resources are not always easy to fund but books need to take priority and

Year 4 children enjoying the humorous 'I Am Not A Loser' by Jim Smith.

be showcased in such a way that they are respected and valued. There are two considerations when trying to develop your school into a *'We love reading'* school. From experience, the schools that do well – with the right ethos and positive messages about reading – adopt many smaller initiatives and strands, and it is the coming together of all of these aspects that has the net result of a big impact. A school's reading culture – and its reading environment – are of equal importance.

Reading culture

Homework

The reading culture needs to be etched across many aspects of school life to show children that we care about reading. In primary schools, one of the most important strategies is to promote reading at home. A strong, clear homework policy, which prioritises reading, will ensure the community facilitates some of the most crucial learning for driving up results. Parental engagement in children's reading is a more important factor in attainment than parental occupation (*OECD, 2002*). Schools need to make the 'reading record' a highly valued home/ school journal that ensures participation in reading is the most important activity that parents engage in. Parents often become confused by a school's homework policy, that can change from teacher to teacher, and become less vigilant as a year progresses. If reading daily for 10 minutes is the requirement – and this is closely monitored with feedback as well as incentivised – then pupils will value their own engagement in the process. On my

travels, I once met a reading fairy (a class teacher wearing wings), who would check reading records/logs in an ad hoc fashion to see if children had read to a parent/carer the previous night. The reading fairy could only validate entries signed by parents and points were awarded to children who had 'banked' that time. As a reward for reading regularly, pupils' names were entered into a monthly draw to win a book, based on points accrued on reading charts.

Reading records need regular interrogation by teachers to show how much we value pupils' efforts. Parents who are not swamped with homework sheets or junk modelling projects can focus properly on this one aspect. Equally, teachers who are not increasing their marking workload with vast quantities of homework can target their time on fostering a love of reading.

The 'tickled pink' feather duster is used as an effective reward system in this reception class.

Adopt an author

Being an author can be a very lonely occupation and some writers crave time away from their work stations. Many would welcome being adopted by a class. It is, however, always advisable to adopt an author who is still alive (as this makes for a far more rewarding relationship). Once adopted, a class can email him/her regularly, find out more about why and how they write and look out for their new books to review. The adopted author can have a special sign in the classroom and fun facts about them displayed. Some adopted authors might visit the school and provide a workshop about their books – sharing more about their characters, motivations for writing particular stories and their sources of inspiration.

Joanna Nadin, author of *The Step Monster*, was not so much adopted by a pupil as accosted – when the youngster became disillusioned that the author had not abided by the strict grammatical rules in the current national curriculum. This is Isabella's letter, which reveals her disgust at Joanna starting sentences with conjunctions:

> Dear Joanna
> In your book the step monster you start a sentence with the word and. We have been taught not to start with a conjunction. Why have you done this on Page 5?
>
> Yours sincerely
>
> I Sabella Rhodes
> Age.6

Now enjoy Joanna's wonderful reply, soaked sarcastically in a smattering of sentence-opening conjunctions. A great example of an insightful author bending the grammar rules for effect and purpose.

Dear Isabella,

So, first of all I want to say thank you for writing to me. And an even bigger thank you for questioning a rule. Because I am often questioning rules, for example why do men wear ties? And why isn't Robert a girls' name? And why are cats allowed to wander wherever they want but goats aren't? Although actually that last rule makes sense, because goats would eat everything they saw, but the rule on not starting a sentence with 'and' is a silly one. And I can tell you a secret, which is that all of my writer friends, including some super famous ones, do it all the time, and so do magazines, and newspapers, and even Prime Ministers – I know this because I used to write for one, and I made sure he started sentences with 'and' and 'but'. So, next time your teacher tells you that you can't start a sentence with a conjunction, you had probably better do what you're told. But you can also secretly smile to yourself that you know this is a rule you're allowed to break all the time in real life. And you can even change your name to Robert too, if you fancy.

Joanna

* 'Adopt an Author' certificate - see Appendix

Love a laureate

The role of *Children's Laureate* is awarded once every two

"Words woven in your secret reading garden will forever flourish." Taken from Jane's speech as she opened this novel space at Long Buckby Junior School, Northampton.

years to an eminent writer or illustrator of children's books – to celebrate outstanding achievement in their field. The first children's laureate was illustrator Quentin Blake in 1999. This came about after a discussion between Ted Hughes (then poet laureate) and Michael Morpurgo, who felt there was a gap in recognition. Outlined below is a capture of laureates through the years:

Quentin Blake 1999–2001

Blake, who is best known for his illustrations in Roald Dahl books, has won many major prizes.

Awards:
Mister Magnolia – *Kate Greenaway Medal (1980)* and the *Red House Children's Book Award (1981)*; **All Join In** – the *Kurt Maschler Award (1990)*; **Clown** – the *Bologna Ragazzi Prize (Italy)* and the

Nestlé Smarties Book Prize (Bronze Award) (both 1996); **The Green Ship** – the *Kurt Maschler Award* and *Nestlé Smarties Book Prize (Bronze Award) (both 1998)*.

Anne Fine 2001–2003

Fine has written more than fifty children's books, including two winners of the annual *Carnegie Medal* and three highly commended runners-up. For some of those five books, she also won the *Guardian Children's Fiction Prize*, a Smarties prize, two *Whitbread awards*, and was twice named *Children's Author of the Year* at the *British Book Awards*.

Awards:
Goggle-Eyes – *Carnegie Medal and Guardian Children's Fiction Prize (both 1990)*; **Bill's New Frock** – *Nestlé Smarties Book Prize, 6-8 years (1990)*; **Flour Babies**

– Carnegie Medal (1993); **The Tulip Touch** – Whitbread Children's Book Award (1996).

Michael Morpurgo 2003–2005

Morpurgo is best known for children's novels such as *War Horse (1982)*. His work is noted for its 'magical storytelling', for recurring themes, such as the triumph of an outsider or survival, and for his characters' relationships with nature.

Awards:
The Wreck of the Zanzibar – Whitbread Children's Book Award (1995); **The Butterfly Lion** – Nestlé Smarties Book Prize (Gold Award) (1996); **Kensuke's Kingdom** – Red House Children's Book Award (2000); **The Last Wolf** – Nestlé Smarties Book Prize (Bronze Award) (2002); **Private Peaceful** – Red House Children's Book Award (2004).

Jacqueline Wilson 2005–2007

Dame Jacqueline's novels for children are frequently themed around delicate topics, such as adoption, divorce and mental illness. Despite this attracting some controversy, she has won many awards including the *Smarties* prize and the *Guardian Children's Fiction Prize*.

Awards:
The Illustrated Mum (1999) — *Guardian Children's Fiction* Prize; *Children's Book of the Year at the British Book Awards* and the *Whitbread* shortlist. **The Story of Tracy Beaker** – *Blue Peter People's Choice Award (2002)*; **Girls in Tears** – *Children's Book of the Year at the British Book Awards (2003)*. **The Story of Tracy Beaker** (1991) and **Double Act** (1995) were both 'Highly Commended' runners-up for the annual Carnegie Medal.

Michael Rosen 2007–2009

Rosen is an avid member of the Twitterati, blogs regularly about English and education and can often be heard on Radio 4 exploring language and poetry. He considered his role as laureate an honour:

Books by Laureates are extra special. Discovering the power of the visual in Anthony Browne's imaginative picture books.

"Sometimes when I sit with children, when they have the space to talk and write about things, I have the feeling that I am privileged to be the kind of person who is asked to be part of it."

Awards:
You Can't Catch Me – Signal Poetry Award (1982); **We're Going on a Bear Hunt** – Nestlé Smarties Grand Prize (1989); ***Sad Book** – an exceptional award in The English Association's Best Children's Illustrated Books of 2004 (4-11 age range).

Anthony Browne 2009–2011

Browne is an internationally-acclaimed author and illustrator of children's books, with nearly 40 titles to his name. His fantastical works blend ingenious puns with strong, colourful images, offering near-photographic realism. Through skilful use of pattern and background detail, Browne subtly conveys an exquisite empathy for his lonely and sensitive central characters. Gorillas feature regularly in his stories and remind Anthony of his father, a boxer who was muscly and strong, yet sensitive and kind. He believes his love of illustrating gorillas, and making them the main protagonists, reflects his personal love for his father.

"I hope to encourage more children to discover and love reading, but I want to focus particularly on the appreciation of picture books, and the reading of both pictures and words. Picture books are for everybody at any age, not books to be left behind as we grow older. The best ones leave a tantalising gap between the pictures and the words, a gap that is filled by the reader's imagination, adding so much to the excitement of reading a book."

In 2000, Browne scooped the highest international honour for illustration – the Hans Christian Andersen Award – for his services to children's literature. He was the first British illustrator ever to win the prize.

Other awards:
Gorilla (1983) – an unprecedented number of awards including the Kate Greenaway Medal; the Kurt Maschler Award; the New York Times' Best Illustrated Book and The Boston Globe-Horn Book Award. **Zoo** – Kate Greenaway Medal (1992); **Voices in the Park** – the Kurt Maschler Award (1998).

Julia Donaldson 2011–2013

Julia Donaldson is the outrageously talented, prize-winning author of the world's best picture books, with over 65 million books sold worldwide. She collaborates with lots of different and highly talented illustrators. We all know the bold, dramatic cartoon style of Axel Scheffler in The Gruffalo, compared to the softer, chalky approach of Emily Gravett,

---

*This book dealt with bereavement and followed the 2002 publication of Carrying the Elephant: A Memoir of Love and Loss (Penguin), which was published after the death of Rosen's son Eddie from meningitis in 1999. Eddie features in much of Rosen's earlier poetry.

who illustrated the fabulous Cave Baby. Donaldson also writes fiction, poems, plays and songs. **Running on the Cracks** (her 2009 novel for teenagers) won the *Nasen Inclusive Children's Book Award.*

Other awards:

The Gruffalo *– Nestlé Smarties Book Prize (Gold Award) (1999);* **Room on the Broom** *– Blue Peter Best Book to Read Aloud (2003);* **Stick Man** *– Specsavers Bestseller Awards Platinum (2016);* **The Detective Dog** *– Books Are My Bag, Readers Award (2016).*

Malorie Blackman 2013–2015

Blackman has written more than sixty books for children and teenagers. One of the reasons she started writing children's book was:

"I wanted to show black children just getting on with their lives, having adventures, and solving their dilemmas, like the characters in all the books I read as a child."

In March 2014, Blackman joined other prominent authors in supporting the *Let Books Be Books* campaign, which sought the removal of 'for girls' or 'for boys' labelling on children's books. As a result, at least ten major publishers agreed to withdraw gender-specific books.

Awards:
For her body of work – the Children's Book Circle's Eleanor Farjeon Award
(2005); **Pig-Heart Boy** *– Carnegie Medal (shortlist) (1998);* **Noughts and Crosses** *– Red House Children's Book Award (2002);* **Cloud Bursting** *– Nestlé Smarties Book Prize (2004).*

Chris Riddell 2015–2017

Riddell is a writer and illustrator, known for his distinctive line drawings and clever caricatures. His latest book *100 Hugs* gathers powerful quotes and stunning illustrations about family, friends, sadness and love. Through his drawings, the following famous quotes are brought to life:

"Words are easy, like the wind; faithful friends are hard to find."
William Shakespeare

"One word frees us of all the weight and pain of life: that word is love."
Sophocles

"Every heart sings a song, incomplete, until another heart whispers back."
Plato

"Never love anyone who treats you like you're ordinary."
Oscar Wilde

Awards:

Pirate Diary *– Kate Greenaway Medal (2002);* **Jonathan Swift's Gulliver** *– Kate Greenaway Medal (2004);* **Goth Girl** *and* **Ghost of a Mouse** *– Costa Children's Book Award (2013).* In 2015, Riddell won the *Hay Festival Medal for Illustration.*

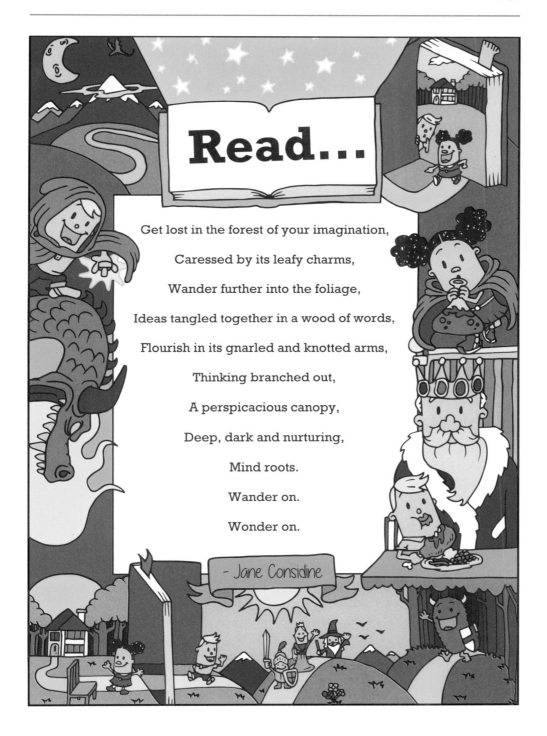

Read...

Get lost in the forest of your imagination,

Caressed by its leafy charms,

Wander further into the foliage,

Ideas tangled together in a wood of words,

Flourish in its gnarled and knotted arms,

Thinking branched out,

A perspicacious canopy,

Deep, dark and nurturing,

Mind roots.

Wander on.

Wonder on.

— Jane Considine

Lauren Child 2017-2019

As this book went to press, award-winning writer and illustrator Lauren Child MBE was appointed *Waterstones Children's Laureate 2017-2019*.

Best-known as creator of the *Charlie and Lola* picture books (later televised on CBeebies) and the *Clarice Bean* series of picture books and novels, Child has also enjoyed success with the *Ruby Redfort* series, about a code-cracking teenage detective.

Speaking at her inauguration ceremony, on the eve of the General Election, Child expressed concern for today's young readers. "There are many children who don't have access to books and they don't have access to books in their schools because a lot of schools don't have libraries," she said. "If we value literacy as much as we say we do, and as much as we should, then children need that opportunity."

Her views echoed those of outgoing laureate, Chris Riddell, who called on the new government to urgently address continuing library closures, which he described as 'a blight on the intellectual development and creative futures of all our children'.

Child, who has an adopted daughter from Mongolia, has also highlighted the problem of white Caucasian children dominating picture book covers, TV shows and films.

Awards:

As a writer:
Clarice Bean, That's Me – *Nestlé Smarties Book Prize Bronze Award, 6-8 years (1999);* **Beware of the Storybook Wolves** – *Nestlé Smarties Book Prize Bronze Award, 6-8 years (2000);* **What Planet Are You From, Clarice Bean?** – *Nestlé Smarties Book Prize (both the Bronze Award, 6-8 years & the Kids' Club Network Special Award in 2001);* **That Pesky Rat** *Nestlé Smarties Book Prize (both the Gold Award, 6-8 years & the Kids' Club Network Special Award in 2002).*

As an illustrator:
I Will Not Ever Never Eat A Tomato – *Kate Greenaway Medal (2000);* **That Pesky Rat** – *Commended, Kate Greenaway Medal (2002).*

Pupil book donation scheme

Some children are fortunate enough to have many books; others have few to none. A pupil donation scheme can be a welcome addition to a school library. Dedicated shelves are provided for pupils to donate books. Inside the front cover, a sticker is placed to show who has donated the book and the date. A message can be written in the book too, if children would like to. Pupils enjoy sharing and it encourages both recycling and charitable gesture. It is a heart-warming way to show that the joy of reading can be gifted to others.

Devoted whole-class reading is an ideal time to promote the pleasure principle of reading.

Sponsorship

Knowledge of the school community helps here, as does a staff member with good organisational skills. Parents and/or business owners can be asked directly for sponsorship – to keep a child reading through the summer holidays. Working on the principle of one book a week, a summer holiday reading pack needs to include six books. Quotes for a *Key Stage 1* and a *Key Stage 2* pack can be obtained from reasonably-priced book sellers, e.g. *The Book People* or *The Works*. If a company/individual agrees to sponsorship, publicity can be offered (e.g. a local newspaper article and/or permission to quote the school scheme in their own company advertising). Books can also be stamped to show recognition to the local company. Pupils considered most in need would be eligible for the reading pack during the holidays and a prize could be awarded in September for the safe return of all the books and a signature to show they had been read.

Book awards

An in-school 'book awards' can be organised, using titles nominated for national prizes. Children on the school panel can decide if they agree with the final nominees. Encourage pupils to read the shortlist and see if they concur with judges nationally. The most prestigious English book awards, both taking place every June, are:

▶ The *CILIP Carnegie Medal* – awarded by children's librarians to an outstanding book for children and young people.
▶ The *CILIP Kate Greenaway Medal* – awarded by children's librarians for outstanding illustrations for children and young people.

Teacher's Book of the Week

Outside the classroom, on a little shelf with twinkling lights, should be the teacher's *Book of the Week*. This should be his/her top recommendation for pupils, who are invited to write a short note as to why they might want to read it. Responses can be posted in a secret ballot-style box – labelled *It could be you!* – and the teacher can then consider all the entries and decide which pupil deserves to be first to read the book.

Daily Jackanory

Teachers use a 10-minute lunchtime slot to run a *Jackanory* club. This is on a rota basis, so each staff member might only be required once every two weeks (depending on the size of the school). During the slot, pupils are invited to the library to hear a whole story (or the beginning of a story as a teaser) and

Showing all pupils just how much reading is valued with this show-stopping story area at New Park Primary School in Liverpool

the teacher is filmed reading it. Videos can be uploaded to the school website, so children can log in from home later to listen to bedtime stories from their favourite teachers. A truly supportive way the school can promote both story-time and reading at home.

Reading assemblies

Assemblies based on 'values' and those that celebrate learning are both worthwhile activities: however, they have contributed to a gradual decline in story-reading assemblies. It could be useful to have an internal discussion about assembly practice, considering if there is at least some time that can be 'ring-fenced' for storytelling. The types of stories that need promoting on a whole-school level should be those with poignant moral messages, which address the rights of children and explore global issues such as education for girls. Amnesty International has written and endorsed many books with broader messages about being a global citizen. Below are some of the most striking and poignant ones that would be ideal for a range of primary school ages:

- ▶ *We Are All Born Free – The Universal Declaration of Human Rights in Pictures* (Amnesty International).
- ▶ *Here I stand – Stories That Speak for Freedom* (Amnesty International).
- ▶ *Dreams of Freedom – In Words and Pictures* (Amnesty International).

- ▶ *Azzi in Between* – the frightening, war-induced journey of a young girl and her family by Sarah Garland.
- ▶ *Dare to be Different – A Celebration of Freedom* by Elana Bergin, Malorie Blackman and Fiona Waters.
- ▶ *Enemy: A Book About Peace* – a profound anti-war book by Davide Cali.
- ▶ *For the Right to Learn – Malala Yousafzai's Story* by Rebecca Langston-George.
- ▶ *The Journey* – a powerful look at the refugee experience by Francesca Sanna.
- ▶ *Refuge – The Timeless Story of Christmas* by Anne Booth and Sam Usher.
- ▶ *One World Together* – travel to nine countries with a little boy by Catherine and Lawrence Anholt.

Assemblies are an ideal time to communally consider our views on aspects of being global citizens.

Reader of the Week

A weekly award with a book as the prize. This is given to the pupil who has consistently read all week and shown excellent comprehension. With agreement from parents, sometimes the *Reader of the Week* could run the *Jackanory* session in the library, showing they are also able to 'read like a teacher'. Their photo can be displayed on an award board and they can have other special duties during that week, e.g. visiting a reception class to read a story and/or helping a teacher listen to younger pupils read.

Blokes, breakfast and books!

In 2012, the *All-Party Parliamentary Group on Literacy* – examining the issue of boys' reading – concluded that the gap was the product of an interplay of factors:

► The home and family environment, where girls were more likely to be bought books and taken to the library, and where mothers were more likely to support children and model reading.

► The school environment, where some teachers had limited knowledge of contemporary/attractive texts for boys, and where boys were not always allowed opportunities to develop their reading identities through reading for enjoyment.

► Male gender identities, which did not value learning and reading as marks of success.

We know there is a clear link between parental involvement and children's educational attainment. Nonetheless, time is a very precious commodity indeed in modern society. In a *National Literacy Trust* survey, men were the ones struggling most to fit in time with their children:

► 82% of men working full-time said they would like to spend more time with their families.

► 74% of fathers said that spending time with their families, or finding time for key relationships, was their biggest life concern.

► 25% of children surveyed said they never saw their father reading.

Launching an initiative to attract more dads, grandads and big brothers into school to promote reading is important. Once a month, class teachers could welcome a male role model to read a story and/or talk about their favourite childhood books. Pupils could then interview the visiting parent, grandparent, sibling or guardian* and ask them interesting questions about life as a child and why they liked particular books.

 One particular school told me volunteers were plentiful when breakfast baps were offered on arrival, which seemed like a good incentive to me.

Book Club

Running a weekly *Book Club* in school (both for Key Stage 1 and Key Stage 2 pupils) is a worthwhile investment. Provide books for all group members, as well as deadlines for finishing each book. Meet the following week, with drinks and biscuits, to discuss the book's strengths and weaknesses, as well as exploring titles with similar themes and deciding which were more successful. Children love reading books that have also been released as films – and debating which they preferred. Designate certain pupils to lead the book club at various times of the year. They will relish the role of 'book expert' and can tailor the 'reads' to the group's interests and passions. Provide assembly time for book club members to enthuse others about their 'reads' and/or announce awards for books read throughout the year. Categories could include: *Most Riveting Read; Most Disappointing Read; Most Side-Splitting Read* etc.

Reading environment

Reading zones

An area in each classroom, as well as spaces around the school, should be designated as fun places to read in. These can be soft, homely spaces – with sofas, soft furnishings and mood lighting – as well as being linked to classroom topics the pupils are studying. On my travels, I have seen some awe-inspiring spaces linked to topics, including a *London Underground* network where pupils could 'get on' at well-known stations and enter well-lit carriages. Other discoveries have included reading caves, jungles, ships and castles. Often, schools that use these well also reward children with reading time. One of my favourite reading zones in a school is called *The Book Nook* – a space where children can kick off their shoes, relax and read.

Reading slippers

The 'slippers' secret came into focus during a study of the physical conditions of classrooms, including temperature, lighting and sound. The *Learnometer* project, a 10-year study by Bournemouth University, found tens of thousands of children worldwide left their shoes outside lessons. It is a prominent practice in most schools in China, India and Scandinavia. Classes where pupils did not wear shoes were much calmer and 95% of pupils read at home with their shoes off.

Project leader, Professor Stephen Heppell, would like to see the 'shoeless' practice in all UK schools – to boost reading enjoyment and academic progress. He also wants to encourage teachers to wear their slippers more often, so as to replicate 'homely' conditions in schools. Comfortability and relaxing for reading go hand in hand and children left to their own devices would not naturally choose to read in upright chairs with their shoes on. At Creaton Primary School in Northamptonshire, pupils win reading time in relaxed zones where they are allowed to remove their shoes. Wearing

All aboard 'The Huddle'! South End Junior School has created a bright and enticing reading zone from a disused bus.

slippers is also a great way to promote both calmness and reading. Every pupil at Pytchley Primary School, also in Northants, has a pair of reading slippers in school. They are allowed to wear them when engaged in any reading activities, whether that be reading to the teacher, guided reading or listening to the class story. A great excuse to get your slippers on!

was made from four double beds, pushed together and dressed with an enormous blanket (lovingly made by the PTA) and about twenty scatter cushions. Every teacher in the school had timetabled slots to use the bed. What was so wonderful about it, was that it seated a whole class of 30 pupils – a fabulous space for children to listen to stories read by their teachers.

The reading bed

As concerns rise about the death of the bedtime story, one of the most fabulous features I have ever seen is an enormous 'reading bed' at the back of a school hall. It

The reading bus

Can you get your hands on a bus? Nag the local bus company for an out-of-service vehicle destined for the scrapyard? If you do manage to acquire one, and it has a working handbrake, then perfect! A bus doesn't require extra planning permission: it can be parked on the school grounds and an enthusiastic PTA can transform it into a library/reading zone that stores books and creates a novel space for reading. It can even serve as a wonderful spot of shelter during a wet playtime. Look at this fabulous bus at South End Junior School in Rushden, Northamptonshire! (top of previous page). It was transformed into *The Huddle* – and makes the perfect statement about the school's commitment to reading space, time and provision.

The school library

"A library in the middle of a community is a cross between an emergency exit, a life raft and a festival. They are cathedrals of the mind; hospitals of the soul; theme parks of the imagination. On a cold, rainy island, they are the only sheltered public spaces where you are not a consumer, but a citizen instead. A human with a brain and a heart and a desire to be uplifted, rather than a customer with a credit card and an inchoate 'need' for 'stuff'. A mall – the shops – is a place where your money makes the wealthy wealthier. But a library is where the wealthy's taxes pay for you to become a little more extraordinary instead. A satisfying reversal. A balancing of the power."
Caitlin Moran, Columnist, The Times Magazine (2011)

School libraries must be vibrant, up to date, organised and well stocked. I have visited some jaw-droppingly delicious libraries that have stopped me in my tracks. The huge, illuminated peach tree in the middle of Kingsley Primary School, Northants, is an installation that lingers in your mind. If possible, a library should be beautiful but actually any library at all is good enough. Some of the modern twists I have seen in school libraries include:

It's a wrap! Don't judge a book by its cover. A message of intrigue might tempt you.

A well-stocked library is appealing to all pupils, even Year 6 boys.

▶ Instrumental music playing at a soothing level;

▶ A reading chair positioned in a carpeted area, with a flamboyant storytelling scarf to encourage pupils to sit in the chair and read to their friends;

▶ Charlie Bucket-style *Golden Tickets* hidden inside books for lucky pupils to discover.

Ways to make the ordinary more interesting

There are many ways we can make school libraries more enticing and intriguing:

▶ **Quick book reviews** – laminate speech bubbles and attach photographs of staff members and pupils. Encourage staff to complete book reviews and attach them to the relevant books, with covers displayed on the tops of bookshelves. Pupils will be interested to see their favourite teachers' opinions and will enjoy taking recommendations from their peers.

▶ Author of the Month – choose an author and display interesting facts and quotes. Gather their books together in a display and let visitors know if they have won any awards. Show clips from *YouTube* of them talking about their books and why they write. Keep an annual calendar of previously featured authors and announce the most popular one at the end of the year.

▶ Blurb bingo – set up a library competition every month where pupils have to guess 10 book titles just from the blurbs. Suggestions can be given as multiple choice answers, with a final open-ended question they have to guess correctly. Entries can be submitted to a competition box and winners announced in assembly. If you have a school book club, some of the older members can help write the competitions.

▶ It's a wrap! – wrap up books in brown paper and string, so pupils meet books they wouldn't normally choose themselves. You can add labels to tempt particular readers, e.g. 'For fans of fast-paced action adventure', or leave the labels off – so pupils experience a range of genres. Age groups are necessary for this type of borrowing to be successful. Hopefully, pupils will be pleasantly surprised with their blind dates!

Blog

A weekly class blog is a superb way of celebrating the reading successes of your class, including the wonderful things children have said about books, their personal reading achievements and/or their notable interests. Please read this endearing blog by Jon Biddle that demonstrates his detailed understanding of how each of his pupils feels about reading, alongside his obvious promotion of reading for pleasure. You are advised to take a deep breath before you start!

Dear Deer Class,
Today I realised something very exciting! Did you know that you're all readers now, every single one of you? I don't mean that you all can read, because you've been able to do that since you were in Reception and Year One. That's a different kind of reading, working out what all the sounds are and how to put them together. I mean that you're readers; real, genuine, passionate readers. I spent a lot of time thinking about it on my way to school this morning (there was bad fog so I had to drive very slowly), and I'm going to try and show you that I'm right.

You're readers because you remind me every single time I forget about you sharing our Poem of the Day. You're readers because you work brilliantly together to tidy up before story time, which means that you can squeeze every last minute out of it.

You're readers because you all get excited whenever a new book arrives in the classroom. You're readers because you work so hard to keep the school library up and running. You're readers because you love talking about your favourite books at every possible opportunity. You're readers because you want to share the books you enjoy with children lower down the school.

In fact, now that I've started, let me be even more specific...

Lauren, you're a reader because as soon as you found out that there was another book written by Katherine Rundell, you marched straight down to the school library to find it.

Troy, you're a reader because you think very carefully about which picture book you're going to share with the children in Reception at story time.

Liam, you're a reader because you love looking at books with beautiful illustrations and trying to recreate them.

Charley, you're a reader because you got so emotionally involved when we read **One Dog and His Boy** together and sat there with tears streaming down your face.

Isobel, you're a reader because you squealed with joy when you found out that there might be a third *Varjak Paw* book one day.

Nico, you're a reader because you insisted that your mum read **Wonder** straight after you did, so that she could see what you were so excited about.

Gracie, you're a reader because you spend every spare minute talking about

how amazing you think Lyra Belacqua and Katniss Everdeen are.

Rubie, you're a reader because you read the books that you enjoy and you don't care what anyone else thinks about them.

Hollie, you're a reader because you spend your playtimes reading the Eddie poems by Michael Rosen to anyone who'll listen.

Jack, you're a reader because you love sending the class photos on Twitter of the purchases you make at the different bookshops you visit.

Andrew, you're a reader because you can recall almost every record from **Guinness World Records 2017** and you know straight away where to find any that you're not sure of.

Alfie, you're a reader because you can remember exactly what happened on page 264 of **Harry Potter and the Goblet of Fire** (and on any page of any other Harry Potter book).

Marley, you're a reader because you've read so many books and you're always happy to share recommendations with your friends.

Layla, you're a reader because you can give a detailed plot summary of every Jacqueline Wilson book ever published.

Oliver, you're a reader because you've been quietly working your way through the **Young Samurai** series since September.

James, you're a reader because you love finding out extra facts about whatever topic we're studying, and you start virtually every sentence with 'Did you know…?'

Romy, you're a reader because you always want to try books that you shouldn't really be reading quite yet. Don't worry, their time will come…and when it does, you'll love them even more.

Leo, you're a reader because you carefully take your signed Tom Palmer book out of your drawer and sit reading it with a contented smile on your face.

Jack, you're a reader because you're not afraid to change a book that you're not enjoying.

Gabriella, you're a reader because you read **Bridge to Terabithia** time and time again. It's wonderful that you enjoy it so much!

Christian, you're a reader because you come in every morning (without fail!) and tell me about the latest developments in the **Once** series.

Sonny, you're a reader because you turn up at school book council meetings absolutely full of fantastic suggestions about which books we can buy for the school.

James, you're a reader because, after a whole year of reading nothing but **Beast Quest**, you were brave and tried the **Ranger's Apprentice** books and **The Hobbit**. And Christian was right, you loved them!

Taylor, you're a reader because you discovered the **Barnaby Grimes** books by Chris Riddell and are happy to tell everyone you meet about how exciting you think they are.

Maddison, you're a reader because you got so angry and frustrated during 'that' chapter in **Wonder**.

Have I proved my point Deer Class? I really hope so. Thinking about all of this today meant that it was the most heart-warming and enjoyable drive to school that I've had for a very long time, so thank you all!

Mr Biddle

Pupils enjoy celebrating their reading journeys.

Consider

The suggestions in this chapter and discuss, during a staff meeting, those that interest you as a school. Talk about the top five strategies that could be employed next - to further strengthen your school as a strong reading community. A mix of both reading culture and reading environment strategies needs to be developed, so that the broader messages about the reading curriculum are positive and are celebrated publicly. It is the coming together of the little things and the big things that shows pupils we really do care about reading.

School Impact Points

Draft out an action plan with timelines and think about how your school would launch any of these initiatives. Try to pair up with a local college/university on a project to market your approach to the pupils and/or parents. Consider how you would monitor and evaluate the effectiveness of your chosen initiatives. Ensure that a display board, seen by many visitors, is used to promote the pleasure principle of reading. This board can have a 'scrapbook' feel to it, with many photographs, reviews, authors' quotes, feelings about reading and the community's views on why reading is so important.

Maarihas, Year 6, Age 10

What Are The Three Zones Of Reading?

"The ideas locked in reading help us to look around new worlds, look inside new people and experience things we might never get the time or chance to."

Chapter 3

Summary

☑ Nationally, pupils demonstrate weaknesses in the following areas of reading:

① Structuring their ideas and having large enough repertoires of vocabulary.

② Communicating their understanding of texts.

③ Analysing at greater depth – when evidence needs gathering from across a text.

☑ Awareness of these deficits means we can deal with th issues 'head on', using *the three zones of reading* to strengthen pupils' abilities to articu ate their own thinking about texts. If we can ensure pupils are competent across all three zones, then they will be excellent readers who can understand, comprehend and analyse texts.

What Are The Three Zones Of Reading?

An overview of the three zones is given here, with more detailed exploration offered in *Chapters 6, 7 and 8.* The three zones of reading are:

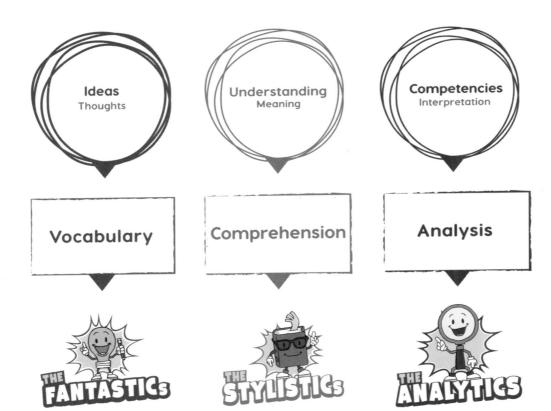

The ideas of reading

"Adolescents entering the adult world in the 21st century will read and write more than at any other time in human history. They will need advanced levels of literacy to perform their jobs, run their households, act as citizens, and conduct their personal lives. They will need literacy to cope with the flood of information they will find everywhere they turn. They will need literacy to feed their imaginations so they can create the world of the future. In a complex and sometimes even dangerous world, their ability to read will be crucial."
The International Reading (now Literacy) Association
Moore et al (1999)

To foster these advanced literacy skills, there is no doubt pupils will have to be excellent readers. Widespread agreement has emerged around the key characteristics of proficient readers, first outlined by Baumann and Duffy in 1997. Good readers are:

► mentally engaged

► motivated to read and learn

► socially active around reading texts

► coordinating a range of comprehension strategies to control the reading process

I am going to summarise the above four strands as *Active skills in reading*.

Pupils enjoying the fantastic cat imagery in *Lion Boy* by Louisa Young.

Active skills in reading

I have often thought one of the most difficult aspects of reading analysis, which children are expected to master, is considering the inner thoughts of a writer. This is an enormous ask for any child – and becomes increasingly important as they move through *Key Stage 2*. Pupils are expected to infer the intentions of the writer, acquire concepts, appreciate the grammatical structure of the writing and place all of this in the context of a book. Children have so much to consider when meeting new reads, as well as many aspects to orchestrate at the point of reading. *Who wrote it? What is its purpose? What are they trying to communicate? What type of audience is it written for?* They even need a meta-language to simply talk about books, e.g. page, beginning, chapter, adventure, non-fiction, author, genre, etc. All of this is part of an active approach to reading, which should be relentlessly encouraged.

Types of reading

Children also need to be taught that there are many different types of reading:

▶ **Reading aloud** – careful, complete and with voice projection and expression

▶ **Scanning and skimming** – rapid, selective and silent

▶ **Critical reading** – underlining sections, making notes, adding questions, marking, highlighting

▶ **Proof reading** – checking for errors, noticing edits required

▶ **Reading for learning** – close reading, slower, inwardly considering

▶ **Reading for pleasure** – own chosen style, mid-paced and the choice to read more/less

In the words of Philip Pullman, author of the fantasy trilogy *His Dark Materials*:

"And we are active about the process...We can skim or we can read it slowly; we can read every word, or we can skip long passages; we can read it in the order it presents itself, or we can read it in any order we please; we can look at the last page first, or decide to wait for it; we can put the book down and... we can assent or we can disagree."

We know that pupils are now reading many different types and styles of text, with considerable change over the last three years. Although they might well be enjoying their reading more, the quality of reading material is not high for some of these popular subsections.

Children who read very little do not enjoy the subsequent benefits: increased vocabulary, greater empathy, positive reading attitude and knowledge of the world. Studies show that when struggling readers are not motivated to read, their opportunities to learn decrease significantly, *e.g. Baker, Dreher and Guthrie (2000)*. This can lead to strong negative feelings about reading and create a vicious circle in which poor readers remain poor readers – *Juel (1988) and*

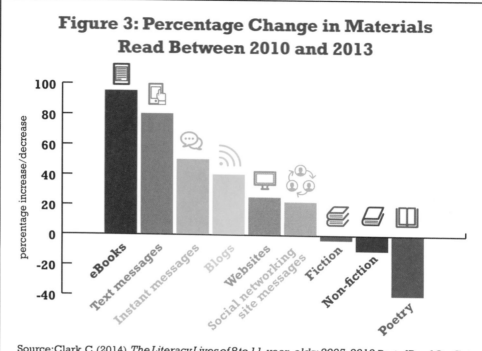

Figure 3: Percentage Change in Materials Read Between 2010 and 2013

Source: Clark, C. (2014), *The Literacy Lives of 8 to 11-year-olds: 2005-2013*. Part of Read On. Get On. (2014) *How reading can help children escape poverty.*

Alvermann (2001). The divide between rich and poor readers grows wider as struggling readers, by nature, limit their acquisition of new vocabulary. Pupils are under growing pressure to widen their vocabularies and all types of reading will strengthen their relationships with words. One of the biggest challenges pupils face is understanding language in context – and the 2016 reading SAT was heavily slanted towards defining and understanding rarely used words. Pupils' understanding of words was defined by *Dale (1965)* on a linear scale:

1. Have never seen it before – no idea

2. Have heard it before but don't know what it means – familiar but unsure

3. Recognise it in context as having something to do with... – good guess

4. Know this well – explains in detail

Handbook of Reading Research Volume 3: Michael L. Kamil, Peter B. Mosenthal, P. David Pearson & Rebecca Barr.

Wesche (1997) added a fifth to this list:

5. I can use this word in a sentence – brings to current vocabulary/usage

A great deal of vocabulary knowledge can be gained incidentally from context. This is further strengthened when mediated by teachers, providing definitions in the context of sentences just read. Words in their natural contexts often reveal meaning; however, the ultimate mechanism for building pupils' language repertoires continues to be reading. This, coupled with teacher explanations, helps pupils to see how language functions.

If, for example, pupils read in a text: *'Carlos could hear the soft, distant symphony of rushing wind'.*

Definitions of individual words would only take pupils' understanding so far. Figurative language often creates challenges for pupils, as comparisons are revealed in unusual ways. The nuances of language need explaining here – namely, the multiple layers of sound made by the wind being akin to a coordinated collection of instruments. For pupils, it is about the linking of ideas to yield meaning within an entire sentence. Interconnectedness is key in reading: when making a point, pupils will often need to draw evidence from various parts of a text. A common mistake is to believe only one quote is needed to support an idea. In reality, writers weave meaning, like silken threads, throughout

a text. Of course, pupils do have to start with what they understand, taking a leap into 'good guess' territory as they grapple for higher level meaning.

The FANTASTICs

FANTASTIC is an acronym that captures the nine ideas of reading. It stands for:

Feeling

Asking

Noticing

Touching

Action

Smelling

Tasting

Imagining

Checking

These are the nine lenses through which writers communicate their ideas. They act as channels for information and include:

▶ **The five senses:** *Noticing (i.e. seeing); Touching; Smelling; Tasting and Checking (or hearing).*

▶ **Two explicit lenses:** *Action (events) and Asking (dialogue/speech).*

▶ **Two implicit lenses:** *Imagining (thoughts) and Feelings (emotions and internal dialogue).* These two lenses help us to focus on characters' unique personalities and motivations.

Writers have only these nine modes at their disposal. Once pupils are introduced to the FANTASTICs in reading, they are able to identify the ideas of reading and the choices writers have made to explore those ideas. It is easier to identify – at sentence level – if a writer has chosen to describe, for example, sounds, smells or feelings. This can provide a powerful link between reading and writing. Knowing that writers have nine potential options, through which to push their ideas, means that reading can be categorised – and pupils are then able to translate knowledge of those classifications into their writing.

Awareness of the FANTASTICs also enables pupils to learn new vocabulary, as well as grouping and sorting words more effectively. Essentially, there are too many words in the English language to prize them out individually and teach them one by one. Pupils needs an easy-to-understand system to group and categorise language – and this is where the FANTASTICs can be brought to bear.

Year 6 pupil sharply focused on reading to discover action in the plot.

A colourful, enticing reading tent at Leyburn Community Primary School. Wider reading builds richer language.

Pupils need to be absorbed in rich, challenging reads, which demand sifting and sorting of language according to ideas. Banks of words acquired during reading experiences can easily be classified into these nine component ideas, helping pupils to see the connections in language. Active readers must take responsibility for building their own personal vocabularies. If children have a method for filing, grouping and organising new words/phrases, their understanding will rapidly accelerate. With a growing vocabulary comes strengthened thinking and the confidence to experiment with more nuanced ideas. It is paramount that pupils are able to see how vocabulary enables writers/readers to explore ideas within a particular lens.

Miller and Wakefield (1993) argued that pupils acquired 2,000 new words a year on average up until adulthood. Being a poor or reluctant reader puts a serious dent in this quantity. Vocabulary growth is exponentially linked to reading quantity and quality. Once we have pupils hooked on books, we can be assured they will amass a wealth of words to deploy down the line in their own writing.

The understanding of reading

Reading comprehension is the ability to decode text, process it and understand its meaning. An individual's ability to comprehend text is influenced by his/her traits and skills, one of which is the ability to store and retrieve previous information to compile a sequence of events. If word recognition is difficult, students use too much of their processing capacity to read individual words, which interferes with their ability to understand and 'take in' words for meaning. Comprehending is tricky in itself – and it is made even trickier when pupils have to explain their thinking. In a two year longitudinal study of 90 British children, beginning at school entry point, researchers discovered three literacy aspects that were predictors of how well pupils could comprehend reading materials by the end of Year 2. These were: word recognition skills, vocabulary knowledge and grammatical knowledge. Where these were strong, pupils were particularly adept at reading comprehension.

During reading activities, when pupils need to demonstrate understanding, they are involved in a process that requires them to simultaneously:

▶ interact with the text

▶ extract information from it

▶ construct their own views about it

This is not a simple process. Pupils need to be made aware of the many ways a text can be interrogated.

STYLISTIC is an acronym that shows pupils the many different layers that exist in a text.

Some are more obvious than others, requiring 'zoom in' reading strategies, such as identifying the central character or where a story is set. Others are 'zoom out' reading strategies that require a broader knowledge of the text – to assess strands and aspects that are echoed in different places (e.g. themes). The STYLISTICs allow children to read purposefully, considering the text with regard to the specific aspect(s) being interrogated.

The competencies of reading

The challenge of teaching reading comprehension is heightened in the current educational era, with children expected to read a wider range of texts that are also more complex. To be prepared for the high-stakes reading SAT, pupils need particular help when it comes to evaluating authors, comparing texts, considering their effectiveness and deciding whether or not they were successful in relation to the writer's intent. Reading comprehension requires maturity, as well as the capacities, abilities, knowledge and experiences that a child brings to the act of reading. Prior knowledge is invaluable to readers when they need to summarise, compare or make judgements. ANALYTICS is an acronym representing the higher order skills of reading, such as inferring, deducing and making predictions:

- Author Assessment
- Navigating Genres
- Accessing Phonics & Grammar
- Language
- Your Personal Opinions

- Trawling for Evidence
- Inferring/Deducing
- Considering Deeper Messages
- Stating Predictions

Pupils need to develop their identities as readers. They need to foster their own reading awareness, as well as honing their active reading skills. A useful term to use in primary schools is 'book detective'.

Book detectives

Book detectives have the following skills and attributes. They:

1. Read in an alert way.

2. Think hard about reading.

3. Can follow lines of enquiry.

4. Investigate thoroughly.

5. Are always on the lookout for clues.

6. Put together smaller pieces of evidence to draw conclusions.

In studies, pupils who perceived themselves as good readers, and in turn

We are BOOK DETECTIVES

Read in an alert way

1

Think hard about reading

2

Can follow lines of enquiry

3

Investigate thoroughly

4

Put together smaller pieces of evidence to draw conclusions

6

Are always on the lookout for clues

5

were assessed as able readers, displayed four characteristics that differentiated them from poorer readers:

► positive attitude about the reading process and goals for reading

► recognition of aspects of text structure

► use of general knowledge, personal experiences, and associations

► responses in *extensive* rather than reflexive mode, meaning they focussed on understanding the author's ideas, rather than directing their attention towards themselves and their own personal thoughts and feelings.

Block (1986); Brown, A.L. (1982); Clay (1979).

More mature readers react in *extensive mode*, by integrating information and monitoring their understanding consistently and effectively. It is clear that pupils need to regularly practise reading, as part of a positive experience, and reflect closely on the reading material. This enables them to build general knowledge as well as empathy for others through reflecting outwardly.

Being a book detective and finding evidence is a crucial component of reading for comprehension.

Consider

Asking pupils to rank school-based reading activities on a positivity index, where 0 = not at all positive, 1 = slightly positive, 2 = positive and 3 = extremely positive.

► Visiting the school library

► Reading 1:1 to a teacher

► Reading aloud in class

► Listening to the teacher read a story

► Reading with a group of other pupils

► Meeting authors

► World Book Day

School Impact Points

Discuss findings from the pupils' positivity index and reflect on reading situations and experiences that pupils enjoyed the most and least. Building on research, which shows that pupils with positive reading attitudes enjoy and develop their reading further, explore how the school's reading provision can be developed and strengthened to maximise positive reading opportunities for pupils.

Dylan, Year 2, Age 6

How Can The Reading Rainbow Help Us Teach Reading?

"Somewhere within the rainbow,
Knowledge grew,
And the skills that you cared to develop,
Really did come through."

Chapter 4

Summary

The Reading Rainbow:

☑ is a visual overview of <u>all</u> reading competencies for primary-aged pupils

☑ is organised into three layers (covering simpler, intermediate and higher order skills)

☑ supports the delivery of reading sessions by enabling teachers to focus on one 'lens' at a time through differentiated reading experiences.

☑ is a supportive construct for developing a broad repertoire of skills in pupils of all ages.

HOOKED ON BOOKS

How Can The Reading Rainbow Help Us Teach Reading?

The *Reading Rainbow* is a capture of all the necessary primary reading domains and competencies. The three layers, from top to bottom, cover:

1. The ideas of reading: FANTASTICs

2. The understanding of reading: STYLISTICs

3. The competencies of reading: ANALYTICS

Through deploying each of the *Reading Rainbow* lenses, pupils will become more confident explorers of a range of text types, including stories, non-fiction and poetry. In fact, it supports every age group – from Foundation Stage all the way up to Year 6 – with early feedback suggesting:

▶ teachers really appreciate having a one-page visual summary of all the required skills.

▶ it supports whole-school continuity and progression, being suitable for every age group and instantly providing a shared language for teachers to discuss reading.

The rainbow is layered in a hierarchical fashion, with the easiest aspects of reading (FANTASTICs) on the top layer, the mid-range concepts (STYLISTICs) on the second layer and the higher level skills (ANALYTICS) at the bottom. Already used by hundreds of teachers around the UK, it fulfils all the requirements of the current national curriculum and brings clarity to the business of driving up whole-school standards in reading comprehension.

F	**A**	**N**	**T**
Feeling	Asking	Noticing	Touching

S	**T**	**Y**	**L**
Setting	Text layout/ Structure	Yes/No Relationships	Logical Meaning Making

A	**N**	**A**	**L**
Author Assessment	Navigating Genres	Accessing Phonics & Grammar	Language

Readir

A	S	T	I	C
Action	Smelling	Tasting	Imagining	Checking

I	S	T	I	C
Interrogating Facts/Opinions	Solving Problems	Themes	Impact	Characters

Y	T	I	C	S
Personal Opinions	Trawling for Evidence	Inferring/Deducing	Considering Deeper Messages	Stating Predictions

Rainbow

What are the national curriculum requirements for primary reading?

Year 1 programme of study

Reading – word reading

Statutory requirements

Pupils should be taught to:

- apply phonic knowledge and skills as the route to decode words
- respond speedily with the correct sound to graphemes (letters or groups of letters) for all 40+ phonemes, including, where applicable, alternative sounds for graphemes
- read accurately by blending sounds in unfamiliar words containing GPCs that have been taught
- read common exception words, noting unusual correspondences between spelling and sound and where these occur in the word
- read words containing taught GPCs and –s, –es, –ing, –ed, –er and –est endings
- read other words of more than one syllable that contain taught GPCs
- read words with contractions [for example, I'm, I'll, we'll], and understand that the apostrophe represents the omitted letter(s)
- read aloud accurately books that are consistent with their developing phonic knowledge and that do not require them to use other strategies to work out words
- re-read these books to build up their fluency and confidence in word reading.

Reading – comprehension

Statutory requirements

Pupils should be taught to:

▶ develop pleasure in reading, motivation to read, vocabulary and understanding by:

- listening to and discussing a wide range of poems, stories and non-fiction at a level beyond that at which they can read independently

- being encouraged to link what they read or hear read to their own experiences

- becoming very familiar with key stories, fairy stories and traditional tales, retelling them and considering their particular characteristics

- recognising and joining in with predictable phrases

- learning to appreciate rhymes and poems, and to recite some by heart

- discussing word meanings, linking new meanings to those already known

▶ understand both the books they can already read accurately and fluently and those they listen to by:

- drawing on what they already know or on background information and vocabulary provided by the teacher

- checking that the text makes sense to them as they read and correcting inaccurate reading

- discussing the significance of the title and events

- making inferences on the basis of what is being said and done

- predicting what might happen on the basis of what has been read so far

- participate in discussion about what is read to them, taking turns and listening to what others say

- explain clearly their understanding of what is read to them.

Year 2 programme of study

Reading – word reading

Statutory requirements

Pupils should be taught to:

- ► continue to apply phonic knowledge and skills as the route to decode words until automatic decoding has become embedded and reading is fluent
- ► read accurately by blending the sounds in words that contain the graphemes taught so far, especially recognising alternative sounds for graphemes
- ► read accurately words of two or more syllables that contain the same graphemes as above
- ► read words containing common suffixes
- ► read further common exception words, noting unusual correspondences between spelling and sound and where these occur in the word
- ► read most words quickly and accurately, without overt sounding and blending, when they have been frequently encountered
- ► read aloud books closely matched to their improving phonic knowledge, sounding out unfamiliar words accurately, automatically and without undue hesitation
- ► re-read these books to build up their fluency and confidence in word reading.

Reading – comprehension

Statutory requirements

Pupils should be taught to:

▶ develop pleasure in reading, motivation to read, vocabulary and understanding by:

- listening to, discussing and expressing views about a wide range of contemporary and classic poetry, stories and non-fiction at a level beyond that at which they can read independently

- discussing the sequence of events in books and how items of information are related

- becoming increasingly familiar with and retelling a wider range of stories, fairy stories and traditional tales

- being introduced to non-fiction books that are structured in different ways

- recognising simple recurring literary language in stories and poetry

- discussing and clarifying the meanings of words, linking new meanings to known vocabulary

- discussing their favourite words and phrases

- continuing to build up a repertoire of poems learnt by heart, appreciating these and reciting some, with appropriate intonation to make the meaning clear

▶ understand both the books that they can already read accurately and fluently and those that they listen to by:

- drawing on what they already know or on background information and vocabulary provided by the teacher

- checking that the text makes sense to them as they read and correcting inaccurate reading

- making inferences on the basis of what is being said and done

- answering and asking questions

- predicting what might happen on the basis of what has been read so far

▶ participate in discussion about books, poems and other works that are read to them and those that they can read for themselves, taking turns and listening to what others say

▶ explain and discuss their understanding of books, poems and other material, both those that they listen to and those that they read for themselves.

Year 3 and 4 programme of study

Reading – word reading

Statutory requirements

Pupils should be taught to:

► apply their growing knowledge of root words, prefixes and suffixes (etymology and morphology) both to read aloud and to understand the meaning of new words they meet

► read further exception words, noting the unusual correspondences between spelling and sound, and where these occur in the word.

Reading – comprehension

Statutory requirements

Pupils should be taught to:

► develop positive attitudes to reading and understanding of what they read by:
  ▪ listening to and discussing a wide range of fiction, poetry, plays, non-fiction and reference books or textbooks
  ▪ reading books that are structured in different ways and reading for a range of purposes
  ▪ using dictionaries to check the meaning of words that they have read
  ▪ increasing their familiarity with a wide range of books, including fairy stories, myths and legends, and retelling some of these orally
  ▪ identifying themes and conventions in a wide range of books
  ▪ preparing poems and play scripts to read aloud and to perform, showing understanding through intonation, tone, volume and action
► discussing words and phrases that capture the reader's interest and imagination
► recognising some different forms of poetry (for example, free verse, narrative poetry)
► understand what they read, in books they can read independently, by:
  ▪ checking that the text makes sense to them, discussing their understanding and explaining the meaning of words in context
  ▪ asking questions to improve their understanding of a text
  ▪ drawing inferences such as inferring characters' feelings, thoughts and motives from their actions, and justifying inferences with evidence
  ▪ predicting what might happen from details stated and implied
  ▪ identifying main ideas drawn from more than one paragraph and summarising these
  ▪ identifying how language, structure, and presentation contribute to meaning
► retrieve and record information from non-fiction
► participate in discussion about both books that are read to them and those they can read for themselves, taking turns and listening to what others say.

Year 5 and 6 programme of study

Reading – word reading

Statutory requirements

Pupils should be taught to:

- ▶ apply their growing knowledge of root words, prefixes and suffixes (morphology and etymology), both to read aloud and to understand the meaning of new words that they meet.

Reading – comprehension

Statutory requirements

Pupils should be taught to:

- maintain positive attitudes to reading and understanding of what they read by:
  - continuing to read and discuss an increasingly wide range of fiction, poetry, plays, non-fiction and reference books or textbooks
  - reading books that are structured in different ways and reading for a range of purposes
  - increasing their familiarity with a wide range of books, including myths, legends and traditional stories, modern fiction, fiction from our literary heritage, and books from other cultures and traditions
  - recommending books that they have read to their peers, giving reasons for their choices
  - identifying and discussing themes and conventions in and across a wide range of writing
  - making comparisons within and across books
  - learning a wider range of poetry by heart
  - preparing poems and plays to read aloud and to perform, showing understanding through intonation, tone and volume so that the meaning is clear to an audience
- understand what they read by:
  - checking that the book makes sense to them, discussing their understanding and exploring the meaning of words in context
  - asking questions to improve their understanding
  - drawing inferences such as inferring characters' feelings, thoughts and motives from their actions, and justifying inferences with evidence
  - predicting what might happen from details stated and implied
  - summarising the main ideas drawn from more than one paragraph, identifying key details that support the main ideas
  - identifying how language, structure and presentation contribute to meaning
- discuss and evaluate how authors use language, including figurative language, considering the impact on the reader
- distinguish between statements of fact and opinion
- retrieve, record and present information from non-fiction
- participate in discussions about books that are read to them and those they can read for themselves, building on their own and others' ideas and challenging views courteously
- explain and discuss their understanding of what they have read, including through formal presentations and debates, maintaining a focus on the topic and using notes where necessary
- provide reasoned justifications for their views.

The *Reading Rainbow* makes the teaching of reading both manageable and meaningful. With nine 'lenses' on each layer, the generic nature of the design is its strength: it serves as a useful prompt for rich and varied interactions with a variety of books and text types. For teachers, the rainbow provides a framework for probing questions, such as *how? why? what if?* and *how do you know?*, and pupils are far more likely to remember learning that is focused through the lenses. Assessment can also be linked to the *Reading Rainbow*, with teachers able to collate summative and formative information about pupils engaged in reading activities in 'real time'.

The *Reading Rainbow* really appeals to children too. Through its simple, eye-catching graphics, they can easily relate to the summarised information. In fact, with so many abstract concepts for pupils to navigate, it's not surprising they embrace these concrete representations along the pathway to becoming proficient readers. It supports pupils in structuring their answers and elicits high order sentence structures that demonstrate deep understanding.

Each of the lenses explained

All of the lenses can be applied to both stories and non-fiction. Some lenses will be less appropriate for poetry, but this really depends on the types of poems being explored in class. Teachers can use their discretion to choose the appropriate lens/lenses for each genre.

FANTASTIC Layer

Feeling

This reading lens focuses on the emotions in a text. It helps pupils to identify key feelings experienced by the central character and consider whether or not they can personally relate to them. As well as stimulating discussion on evocative moments, this lens encourages pupils to discuss and develop empathy for characters' plights. Emotions of significant people in non-fiction texts can be investigated too.

Asking

The emphasis here is on the oral interactions in a book/text. The central character's conversations are dissected – inspiring discussions about what they expose. Dialogue might function to propel the action forward or to reveal a character's inner thoughts. Readers need to consider *what* characters say, and *how* they say it, as well as thinking about the things they leave unsaid. Quotes from non-fiction books can also be extrapolated here. Pupils might consider how expert opinion is quoted or consider the dialogue features of voices from the past.

Noticing

Characters in stories are often written in first person narrative, which means we begin to see the world through their eyes. When working in this lens, pupils should be considering the perspectives and viewpoints of characters. Equally, this lens encourages awareness of observable aspects that authors let us see through description and imagery.

Touching

Writing is more engaging when it is a multi-sensory experience. The sense of touch is an important lens. Expressing how things feel to the touch is another way that writing can replicate real-life experiences. Children need a rich repertoire of texture words to enable them to explore this lens, *e.g. smooth, rough, bristly, embossed.*

Action

Children should be able to seek out the main action in a story. Identifying and discussing key events helps pupils to connect with what is happening. Memorable aspects are often high intensity, with main characters running and jumping through the plot. However, pupils often need support to notice the smaller – sometimes more revealing – action. The white-knuckle, cliffhanger stuff might be more obvious, but sometimes a more subtle action can expose an important new character trait.

Smelling

This lens is used less frequently by writers. However, when it is used well, the impact is a wonderful, three-dimensional experience for readers. Smells can be very evocative of positive and negative experiences in our lives: a waft of perfume or the nasty whiff of a rotten sandwich. Often neglected, but very powerful, a 'smell' dimension in writing can enhance it to a new level. Identifying how authors use smell – or choose to leave it out – can be an interesting exercise, as can exploring how smells are used to create different moods.

Tasting

It is not always relevant for authors to include a sense of taste. Of course, foodstuffs in a story can be described in such a provocative and enticing way that readers can almost taste them too. Conversely, readers might baulk at the descriptions of horrible tastes, such as burnt toast, lumpy porridge or cold gravy. It is the more subtle 'tastes' that readers need to be on the lookout for – the acrid black smoke from a chimney or the sickly-sweet aroma of candyfloss at a fairground. A higher order skill is identifying the way some writers manipulate the sense of taste and attach it to feelings, *e.g. a taste of fear welled up in his throat*.

Imagining

Good writers allow us a window to the deeper, inner thoughts of their characters. Clever writers create dialogue that we know contradicts a character's actual thoughts/motives. Writing is a mix of expressing the outward behaviours of a character, as well as their internal thinking. Through extensive reading, pupils are able to empathise more closely with central characters as they gain insight into their private thoughts and motivations.

Checking

Crash! Bang! Wallop! Sounds bring a story to life and writers can choose to accentuate certain sounds for effect. Sometimes, pauses and long moments of silence can be even more powerful. Often, the smallest sounds in a story can be magnified to create tension, *e.g. the slow creaking of a door handle*. Awareness of how sounds can create atmospheres and tension promotes meaningful discussion about their positive and negative impacts.

STYLISTIC Layer

Setting

The setting is not only a place but a moment in time. If it is somewhere unusual, unique or unfamiliar, pupils can seek out textual evidence of all the smaller elements used to build a detailed description. Two stories can be set in exactly the same place, but feel completely different because of the words chosen by each writer. Often, the smallest of details – or a powerful word choice – can contribute to building a vivid picture in readers' minds. The time of day can also have a significant impact on the mood created.

Text Layout/ Structure

No text will make sense unless it is structured in a clear way. At the very least, it should have a beginning, middle and end. Pupils need to consider the differences in structure conventions across fiction and non-fiction, *e.g. how headings and subheadings are used to compartmentalise information in some non-fiction text types.* This lens will also help pupils to consider how photographs, graphs and tables are used to break up/group information. As readers, understanding why certain layout features have been chosen – and exploring their effectiveness – is critical.

Yes/No Relationships

This lens helps children to examine key characters' relationships with both friends and enemies. The interplay between individuals, and their motives, is often where tension is created in a story or historical non-fiction event, which makes for intriguing reading. Understanding positive and negative relationships means

pupils can begin to empathise with central characters/significant figures in history and their experiences.

Logical Meaning- Making

Being able to discuss key events – and sequence them – reflects burgeoning comprehension skills. Younger children tend to find this skill more difficult, as they are too focused on decoding to read with the ease and fluency needed to hold up the meaning. Equally, older pupils may be challenged as they meet increasingly complex texts, with hidden aspects and the use of deceit as a deliberate device to cause confusion.

Interrogating Facts/ Opinions

This is an important aspect of becoming a proficient reader, particularly when reading non-fiction. Mature readers are able to distil facts from opinions and recognise that bias and prejudice can sometimes influence writers consciously or subconsciously. When looking at newspapers, it may be useful to consider how journalists deploy strategies that package opinions as facts, or use hyperbole to inflate facts to such a degree they are no longer factual.

Solving Problems

All stories revolve around a problem that has to be resolved. These problems are the central events that hold stories together and create key tension. When they are finally resolved, it brings stories to satisfactory conclusions. Problems can also be seen threaded through non-fiction texts: the focus for a letter, an historical event of the past or a changing environment in a geographical text and how this impacts on local people. Pupils need to identify problems of different types, sizes and challenge and consider how they can be grouped for commonality across stories, *e.g. defeating the enemy*.

Themes

Although the events of a story may be interesting or exciting, a story without a theme is little more than a list of events. A theme is revealed to elicit a universal human connection that enables us to engage our attention in a real way. Many people tend to confuse the theme of a story with the plot. Theme is often described as 'the pulse of a story' that threads through all the writing. Common themes include jealousy, appreciation or loss.

Impact

How effective is the text? What was the author's intended impact on the reader? Did they succeed?
What was the effect on the reader? Pupils need to become familiar with the idea that every text is intended to affect its readers in some way. Every reader is, of course, different too and sometimes a text will affect individuals in ways the writer didn't imagine (or one reader may find a depth that others won't). This is particularly true if the text matches personal experience. A story about bereavement is bound to have a more profound effect on a child who has lost someone close; likewise, a non-fiction text about smoking will be more powerful for a pupil who is concerned about a loved one's health. Noticing the intended effect on the reader is an important skill. Even if something doesn't personally interest, horrify, amuse or persuade you, you need to be able to spot what the writer intended its impact to be.

Characters

The protagonist is the main character in a story: the character that the reader or audience empathises with. It is critical that pupils appreciate the protagonist's 'highs' and 'lows' as they move through the plot points of a story – so they can begin to see their personality revealed through reactions and choices they make at each crossroads. In non-fiction, children can learn about the personalities of significant historical figures (e.g. *Nelson Mandela*) through their decisions and life choices.

ANALYTICS Layer

Author Assessment

Evaluating and reviewing an author's work requires the reader to take a critical stance. A good book review analyses, evaluates and judges the content. The skills needed to assess an author's effectiveness build over time, both through experience and through having more comparable texts to use as benchmarks.

Navigating Genres

Reading texts with knowledge of the conventions of certain genre types means that similarities and differences can be explored in a meaningful way. As a reader, the recognisable features of *science fiction*, *suspense* or *romance* can be identified and considered in relation to what is commonly expected from certain text types. A skilled reader, using their 'writerly eye', should be able to identify common features of fiction and non-fiction text types.

Accessing Phonics & Grammar

Early readers are beginning to evidence 1:1 correspondences, drawing on their developing phonic knowledge to link graphemes and phonemes, decode simple words and recognise a core of known words. More advanced readers begin to yield patterns of meaning from different word classes. Young readers can make good phonic guesses and older readers can make good grammar guesses, *e.g. inserting the word 'leapt' in place of 'lurched'*. As pupils become more proficient readers, they begin to see how writers can manipulate word orders for dramatic effect and also how a particular word/phrase can function in different ways, *e.g. I'll get this round (round = noun) versus The car turned round the corner (round = preposition).*

Language

Through precise language choices and literary devices, an author can create intrigue and interest. Pupils should be encouraged to notice unusual turns of phrase and consider why these word choices were made. Equipping them with correct terminology to discuss writerly devices will help them to explore their impact and effectiveness. The BOOMTASTICs (explained in detail in *The Write Stuff* book) is a comprehensive collection of the poetic and figurative language devices used by authors to create impact and give their work a personal stamp.

Your Personal Opinions

How you respond to a text, and how it engages you and grips your attention, is vital. Pupils should be taught that their opinions are valid and that they are the critical audience for children's authors. Sharing book reviews with other pupils is an excellent activity for young readers – underlining the fact that their personal perspective is a benchmark for others to begin to test out similar or differing viewpoints.

Trawling for Evidence

The 'heart of the matter' for skilled book detectives is: supporting quotes, events' summaries and capturing other data. Lines of enquiry, conclusions or analysis must be packaged and delivered with valid textual evidence. Diligent book detectives are able to collate evidence from different places across a text to justify pertinent points.

Inferring/ Deducing

Think of deduction as taking a lot of information and distilling it down to one fact through a process of reasoning. Deduction is a summary skill, a drawing of a conclusion, an educated guess based on what has been read, *e.g. You work at a hospital, you trained for seven years, you work long hours. I can deduce you are a doctor.* An inference is the opposite: you take one fact/hint and extrapolate it out into several assumptions, *e.g. You are a doctor; therefore, I think you are intelligent, kind, care about people and work in a hospital.* Children need regular opportunities to develop both of these crucial skills.

Considering Deeper Messages

In every story, there is one big idea – the lesson an author wants the reader to learn. Stories often serve as analogies for our own lives. It is not only *Aesop's Fables* that are trying to communicate a moral direction or advice for us. This is one of those 'zooming out' reading strategies that requires pupils to take a broad sweep of the text and draw out summative conclusions about the key message(s).

Stating Predictions

As young readers, children are constantly learning to make predictions as they travel through a text. *What do you think will happen next? Who do you think could save them?* These types of questions help children to monitor their understanding of a story while also thinking ahead to the next part. If a pupil is able to make good and fairly accurate predictions, the chances are that they are comprehending the text well. Exploring good predictions and hypotheses, and recognising when we are surprised/ shocked by a turn of events, is all part of developing maturity as a reader.

A cosy corner, with a few home comforts, can boost children's concentration levels and reading stamina.

Book Talk goes beyond the content domains of the national curriculum to ensure pupils build a rich repertoire of skills and understanding.

"**Books are sometimes windows**, offering views of worlds that may be real or imagined, familiar or strange. **These windows are also sliding glass doors,** and readers have only to walk through in imagination to become part of whatever world has been created or recreated by the author. **When lighting conditions are just right, however, a window can also be a mirror.** Literature transforms human experience and reflects it back to us, and in that reflection we can see our own lives and experiences as part of the larger human experience. Reading, then, becomes a means of self-affirmation, and readers often seek their mirrors in books."

Rudine Sims Bishop
"Mirrors, Windows, and Sliding Glass Doors,"
Perspectives: Choosing and Using Books for the Classroom 6.3 (Summer 1990)

Consider

Sharing the *Reading Rainbow* with all staff members and discussing their understanding of each of the lenses.

Exploring the usefulness of each lens, with regard to both fiction and non-fiction. Sharing definitions from this chapter and assigning further meaning to them in relation to pupil age groups taught.

School Impact Points

① Introduce the *Reading Rainbow* and provide a large display with moveable lenses. Ask pupils to define the meanings of each lens and to arrange them from easiest to most difficult.

② Teachers can also consider the rainbow in terms of pupil strengths and weaknesses and highlight the areas they need bolstering in.

③ It should be noted that pupils require more help with 'zooming out' techniques, such as considering deeper messages and themes, compared to 'zooming in' strategies such as authors' word choices.

Ben, Year 1, Age 5

What Is Book Talk?

"Talking about books, getting excited about books - in fact, having a good old chinwag about books is what *Book Talk* is all about. It's about every pupil getting involved and having their say."

Chapter 5

Summary

- [✓] Book Talk needs to happen daily for 30 minutes.

- [✓] Sessions are differentiated through attainment groups, with each group given an appropriate set of books.

- [✓] Feeding back to the group encourages children to 'talk' in comprehension answers.

- [✓] Language of comprehension words are promoted competitively. If used appropriately, pupils earn points for their Book Talk teams.

HOOKED ON BOOKS

What Is Book Talk?

A system for teaching reading

Book Talk is not a casual thing, although it might appear that way to the untrained eye. A visitor walking into your classroom is likely to find a lively atmosphere, the babble of multiple conversations, little to no writing going on and pupils reading from a range of different books. Chaos you might say. Actually, far from it. *Book Talk* feels relaxed and enjoyable for pupils involved, but is structured in a very clear way.

The benefits of *Book Talk*

1. Differentiated from the outset through ability-linked books.

2. Strengthens comprehension strategies, as pupils 'talk' their structured answers.

3. Plugs gaps in vocabulary, by insisting pupils use the language of comprehension. Cohesive words support the explanation of ideas.

4. Enables children to see how the skills of reading can be applied to multiple contexts.

5. Builds confidence through an interactive process of extracting language and constructing meaning.

Frequency and duration

Book Talk should happen every day in every classroom (from Foundation Stage to Year

The Shape of a Book Talk Session
Steps to Success Shared: Read, Listen, Talk

First reason to read: FANTASTIC

Pupils read: group, individual, pair, communal pair

Book Talk: sentence starter

Feedback from pupils

Second reason to read: STYLISTIC

Pupils read: group, individual, pair, communal pair

Book Talk: sentence starter

Feedback from pupils

Third reason to read: ANALYTICS

Pupils read: group, individual, pair, communal pair

Book Talk: sentence starter

Feedback from pupils

First reason to read	Top layer	FANTASTIC	10 minutes
Second reason to read	Middle layer	STYLISTIC	10 minutes
Third reason to read	Bottom layer	ANALYTICS	10 minutes

Total = 30 minutes

6). Timetabling of sessions is completely at the teachers' discretion: they could be right at the beginning of the school day, after lunch or just before hometime. Half an hour is required for each session and this applies to all age groups. Sessions are split into three 10-minute chunks.

Three reasons to read

The *Reading Rainbow* supports the teaching of *Book Talk* and is used to direct and shape the focus of each 10-minute chunk. Sessions are driven by the three reasons to read (the three layers of the *Reading Rainbow*, see table above).

Teachers can direct pupils to use any of the nine lenses from each layer, but should ensure a breadth of lenses is selected each term. Over time, the aim should be to cover all aspects on the rainbow.

Differences between guided reading and Book Talk

The main weakness with guided reading sessions isn't the leadership from teachers.

Sessions are often rich in pupil talk, with teachers highly skilled at pushing pupils to the edge of their thinking. The problematic aspects tend to be the quality of holding activities given to other pupils, along with the pressure to keep the class quiet so the guided reading group can concentrate. *Book Talk* embraces the best parts of guided reading but ensures all pupils are productively involved in the process.

Differentiating a Book Talk session

For *Book Talk,* every pupil must have a copy of the book. Children sit in reading attainment groups and the classroom is set up in such a way that approximately five groups are created. The teacher begins by announcing the first reason to read and chooses a 'focus group'. He/she works with the focus group to support and assess pupils' reading abilities.

Organisation of book resources

For *Book Talk* to be successful, and work generically for all groups, there needs to be

Reading comprehension approaches which focus on learners' understanding of the text have positive impacts.

a commonality of text types across the class. For example, in a 'fiction' session, all pupils need to be reading stories: the subgenre of those stories is irrelevant. Sessions can be equally successful if all pupils are reading non-fiction, but there cannot be a mix of narrative and non-fiction texts across the room. Equally, poems and poetry anthologies can be used in *Book Talk*, as long as all groups have poems to explore.

Many *Book Talk* schools ensure there is a central storage area, where multiple copies of the same book are arranged in packs. Many sets become unusable because an odd book has been left in a staff member's boot. An amnesty can therefore be helpful before *Book Talk* sessions occur: it's amazing what can materialise from both teachers' and pupils' homes! To maximise on resources, it's also wise not to strictly categorise books into Foundation Stage, Key Stage 1 and Key Stage 2 reads. Many books are interchangeable between age ranges.

Organising the groups

For every 10-minute chunk, there are three possible ways pupils can be organised to read:

 Each team member reads a section each – maybe one or two sentences or a paragraph. Very young children can 'read' the pictures to their friends.

☑ Pairs engage in 'shoulder to shoulder' reading. This keeps noise levels down by preventing the voice projection that occurs when pupils are 'face to face'. Again, this approach relies on turn-taking and some classes will need direction about the quantity to be read by each individual, e.g. two sentences each.

☑ Pupils read in their heads, or if they are younger, 'whisper read' to themselves.

It doesn't matter which approach is used for each 10-minute chunk. A *Book Talk* session can include all three (in any order). Some teachers prefer children to always work in groups; however, it's advisable to ensure pupils understand all three methods from the outset, so they become habitual and valuable time isn't wasted daily on clarifications and 'fussing'. Sometimes, if pupils are reading to themselves, a situation can occur where pupils in the same group finish a 10-minute chunk at different points in a book. A policy of rewinding back to the point reached by the slowest reader curtails racing readers and those trying to 'teacher please'.

Outlined below (and as a visual on page 93) is the broad shape of a 10-minute chunk:

1. The first reason to read is announced by the teacher – a reason from the FANTASTIC layer. Let's say the reason is *Action*. All groups are asked to read their books, noticing particular moments of action.

The 'Reading Rainbow' captures the comprehensive scope of all aspects required to facilitate understanding.

2. The teacher announces, for example, that this will be a 'group' reading session. Each group member reads three sentences, looking out for moments of action. This runs for approximately 7 minutes.

3. During this time, the teacher sits with one group, observing their reading and making assessment notes.

4. The teacher calls the whole class to attention and sets a time period for groups to talk about their findings.

This part of *Book Talk* is tightly structured: to support pupils in framing formal comprehension answers in 'talk'. At this point, a sentence starter is provided (linked to the chosen lens) and answers are formulated in groups. For example:

First reason to read: FANTASTIC (Action)

Sentence starter

We found a big/little action in the text, which was...

Language of comprehension word

reveals

Pupils have the chance to win four team points during every *Book Talk* chunk. Groups are given 2 minutes of talk time to construct their spoken comprehension answers, along with strict rules for structuring them:

1. The sentence starter must be used – 1 point

2. Answers must relate to the group's book – 1 point

3. Textual evidence must be quoted or illustrations explained – 1 point

4. A *Book Talk* bonus point is 'up for grabs' for using language of comprehension words appropriately.

The teacher listens to a couple of groups' feedback and awards points.

This format is repeated for the second (STYLISTIC) layer and third (ANALYTICS) layer – the only variation being if the teacher wishes to introduce either the paired/silent reading methods.

As the week progresses, the teacher sits with a different reading group each day and they become the focus group for detailed assessment notes. Assessment of reading is explored in detail in *Chapter 10*.

Three Reasons to Read

Organising the Groups

1 **FANTASTIC**

2 Read around the group, e.g. two sentences each.

3 Sentence starter provided and discussed:

"We found big/little action in the text, which was ....."

4 Hear feedback from individuals using sentence starter.

1 **STYLISTIC**

2 Read in pairs taking turns, (shoulder to shoulder keeps volume down).

3 Sentence starter provided and discussed:

"Our main character is ..... and a positive/negative thing that happens to them is ....."

4 Hear feedback from individuals using sentence starter.

1 **ANALYTICS**

2 Read individually (either 'whisper reading' or 'in their heads').

3 Sentence starter provided and discussed:

"We think one of the main messages of this book is ....."

4 Hear feedback from indivduals using sentence starter.

Consider

Organising a *Book Talk* trial (one session in a Key Stage 1 classroom and one in Key Stage 2) and noting how pupils respond. Focus on the quality of talk and pupil engagement:

- ☑ Is the 'talk' detailed, rich and comprehensive?
- ☑ What differences can be observed between Key Stage 1 and 2 pupils?
- ☑ Do pupils with better general knowledge cope better with reflecting on the reading material?

School Impact Points

Discuss how *Book Talk* promotes and values the 'pleasure principle' of reading, as well as helping pupils to articulate their ideas, opinions and beliefs. Explore how teachers can enhance the interactions of *Book Talk* groups, pushing thinking forwards with questions such as:

- Can you explain that further?
- Why did you think that?
- Has your opinion changed?
- What is the evidence for that?
- Do you have stronger evidence to support that point?

Set up a staff meeting to explore effective practice and discuss approaches that facilitate rich levels of talk. Consider the benefits of *Book Talk* in strengthening oral interactions between pupils and enhancing their comprehension abilities.

Joseph, Year 4, Age 8

How Can We Teach The Ideas Of Reading?

"Once your mind is stretched with new ideas from reading, it will never regain its original dimensions."

Chapter 6

Summary

☑ Talking frames will shape up pupils' thinking.

☑ Pupils need help moving from 'regurgitation' to analysis.

☑ 'The ideas of reading' is a nine lens approach for examining authors' ideas in detail.

☑ Sentence starters help pupils to 'talk' comprehension answers, which are sophisticated, formal and extensive.

How Can We Teach The Ideas Of Reading?

Pupils need frameworks for both thinking and talking – to push them beyond 'regurgitation' and into analysis. Ultimately, the mission is to have truly independent pupils, who are able to use teacher-modelled structures naturally and autonomously.

In the first instance, teachers need to provide sentence starters that closely replicate written comprehension answers. These starters should have a certain tone and sophistication, challenging pupils towards the ever-increasing standards demanded by the Y6 reading SAT. The benefits of these 'prompts' are extensive: they support pupils' thinking as well as promoting cohesive discussions when exploring texts. Often, pupils struggle

to make sense of a text in logical and methodical ways. They need help with sifting and sorting essential details from less important ones. These sentence starters help pupils to articulate their ideas in structured ways, shaping answers that exhibit both critical thinking and in-depth analysis.

The ideas of reading: FANTASTIC sentence starters

Teaching pupils to interrogate a text through its key ideas brings a sense of logic and control to their early attempts at in-depth analysis. Reading can be overwhelming for children, as authors

During *Book Talk*, pupils have a chance to comprehend the meaning of what is written, such as inferring messages from context.

bring too much to bear through their writing. Many children find it difficult to seek out information that cannot be neatly summed up or plucked easily from the text. The FANTASTIC approach neatly packages every possible writing idea into one of nine child-friendly categories. These groupings enable pupils to take a more systematic approach to reading and mentally organising authors' ideas. Of course, writers don't usually write in neat compartments: it is up to the reader to make sense of a tale/non-fiction text – making connections, considering how ideas interrelate across a text and being proficient enough to choose which aspects work together to create an overall effect. The art of being a good reader is gathering information/ideas that have been woven throughout a text. Often, these many strands are trailed across numerous pages, adding further details or building emphasis. Equipped with the FANTASTICs, pupils' skills can be honed so they are less 'scattergun' in their approach. Answers can be fine-tuned through understanding which lens they are working with and the associated language that will assist them in talking about this aspect. With practice, their answers will be like 'sniper rifles' – targeted, accurate and with clear purpose. Moments worth celebrating are those when pupils begin to manipulate the provided sentence starters, tweaking and changing them to suit their own ends. This is clear evidence that the autonomy of their thinking is developing beyond the supportive structure.

The Ideas of Reading

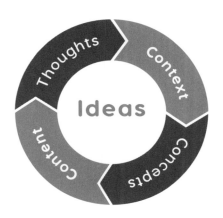

Book Talk provides a clear structure to help pupils orally interact with their peers about the nine ideas for reading.

KS1 FANTASTICs:

♡ Feeling

I feel ...

The character feels ...

Emotions are explored when ...

The pictures tell us ...

The sentence _____ evokes _____ feelings ...

The main emotion/emotions in this book ...

Contrasting emotions are evident when ...

The dominant emotions in this book are ...

Asking

Powerful dialogue is ...

Quotes that are effective are ...

The author uses dialogue to ...

The tone of the character's voice reveals ...

The spoken words of the character tell us ...

The punctuation tells us ...

We find out more about ___ when he/she says ...

The dialogue does/doesn't reveal ...

Noticing

The character sees ...

The character notices ...

As a reader, we can see ...

The author creates a powerful image in our minds by ...

_____ is described in detail because ...

We can see _____ clearly as a reader.

The scene the author presents is ...

The author is unsuccessful in creating images because ...

Touching

The writer leans on the sense of touch when ...

The author rarely uses 'touch' because ...

These are examples of 'touch' words/sentences: ...

The main character is tactile because ...

We sense the character's world when ...

Touch could be used when ...

Touch enhances the reader's experience by ...

The central character touches ...

Action

The main action of the story is ...

_____'s actions reveal ...

Pace is established by ...

Familiar actions of this character are ...

_____'s responses and actions change when ...

This little action shows us ...

An action-packed part of the story is ...

The impact of _____ (insert action) is ...

Smelling

The sense of smell is introduced when ...

The author uses 'smell' to ...

_____(insert smell) evokes ...

If I were to smell the picture, I think it would ...

_____ is an example of a 'smell' word/sentence ...

If I were to smell the scene, I think it would ...

The author uses _____ to arouse our sense of smell ...

Smells are created by the writer when ...

Tasting

Food is important in this story because ...

Food brings characters together when ...

Taste is important during celebrations in the story because ...

Food creates problems/tension by ...

Food is used to symbolise ...

Taste is important in this non-fiction book because ...

The author uses 'taste' sentences to ...

Taste creates atmosphere by ...

Imagining

The character's inner thoughts are revealed when ...

We discovered how this character thinks when ...

Her/His true inner thinking was not revealed because ...

I can imagine what _____ looks like because ...

I think this story is effective because ...

I believe ...

I consider ...

The central ...

Checking/Hearing

Sounds are used to ...

If I were in this story, I would hear ...

The author uses 'sound' effectively when ...

Sound is used by the author to ...

I would add the sense of sound by ...

Onomatopoeia is used when ...

Positive/negative sounds in the story are: ...

_____(insert sound) creates a _____ mood by ...

The 'Reading Thinking Kits' provide oral scaffolds for pupils as they interrogate content through the FANTASTICs.

KS2 FANTASTICs:

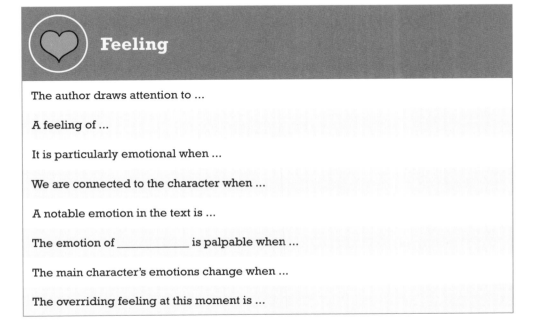

Feeling

The author draws attention to ...

A feeling of ...

It is particularly emotional when ...

We are connected to the character when ...

A notable emotion in the text is ...

The emotion of _____ is palpable when ...

The main character's emotions change when ...

The overriding feeling at this moment is ...

 **Asking**

Significant dialogue in the story is …

_____'s words show us that …

The author uses dialogue to …

We can infer from _____'s spoken words that …

Dramatic dialogue occurs …

The author has deliberately included the spoken words …

The main character speaks more/less than other characters because …

Quotes are used in this non-fiction piece to …

 **Noticing**

We notice more/less than the central character because …

The author heightens the sense of 'sight' through …

We see the world through the main character's eyes when …

Observations made by the central character are revealed through …

Successful aspects in the text help us to visualise …

An image is created in the reader's mind when …

As readers, we can see what is about to befall the central character because …

This non-fiction text organises information to help us see …

Touching

There are negative moments of 'touch' when ...

There are positive moments of 'touch' when ...

The sense of touch is used by the writer to show a relationship with (insert person/object/place) when ...

The writer hasn't explored 'touch' but a missed opportunity was ...

'Touch' is important at this stage of the story because ...

The author brings the environment to life when ...

Touch is seldom used in the text but this small moment reveals ...

The sense of touch is important/unimportant in this non-fiction text because...

Action

We have found a significant/minor action in the story that ...

The action by the central character reflects ...

A gripping, action-packed part of the story is ...

At the moment, the actions in the story are ...

The actions taken by other characters, such as ...

Positive/negative actions are dominant here because ...

A small action that is very telling is ...

The actions of significant people in this non-fiction text show us ...

Smelling

The writer doesn't explore the sense of 'smell' but it could be included when …

Smells in this story could be made more obvious by …

Negative/positive smells are deployed by the author to …

Our impression of _____ could be enhanced by the sense of 'smell' …

The author describes smells in detail, which …

If I were to experience the smells in this story, I think they would be …

Smells that could be associated with the central character are: …

If I were to jump into the pictures/photographs in this non-fiction text, I would smell …

Tasting

Taste is significant/not significant in this story because …

The sense of 'taste' is abundant/non-existent because …

If I'd written this text, I would have included a 'taste' sentence …

Food is used in this text to represent …

The author heightens the sense of 'taste' when …

Positive/negative tastes are deployed by the author to …

Taste is focussed on/not focussed on in this story …

Taste is not referred to in this non-fiction book because …

Imagining

The author lets us inside the central character's mind ...

We learn about the inner thoughts of the character when ...

We can surmise that the inner thoughts of the character are ...

There is a conflict between inner thoughts and direct speech when ...

Our imagination is stretched when we read this story because ...

Personally, I think this book ...

Conflicting viewpoints are represented in this non-fiction text ...

Expert thoughts on the subject matter are shown by ...

Checking/Hearing

The mood evoked in the story through 'sound' is ...

Sounds are emphasised in this part of the story because ...

The author doesn't describe sounds but has missed an opportunity when ...

The sounds change in the story to reflect ...

The sounds heard create calm/tension because ...

The author has chosen to include the sound of _____ because ...

Sounds are revealed in an accurate/poetic way so as to ...

In this non-fiction piece, sounds are described ...

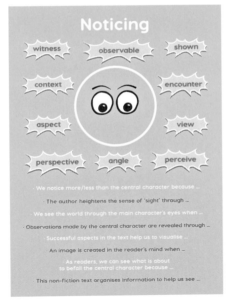

KS1 and KS2 Reading Thinking Kits - The FANTASTICs.
Complete resource available from www.thetrainingspace.co.uk

Consider

Observing pupils using the FANTASTIC sentence starters. Notice if they are able to strengthen their viewpoints through supplementary comments and opinions. What happens when you throw in questions to extend their ideas and thinking?

School Impact Points

Set up a collaborative and supportive network of teachers within and beyond the school. Watch one another teach and provide advice on how to extend pupils' interactions with books. Discuss, as a school, how to develop a strong and effective system that encourages independent reading.

Recognise that a *Book Talk* approach helps foster a level of understanding from pupils that enables them to talk and write about reading material in a meaningful way. Increased sentence talk will drive pupils' development, with sentence starters raising the formality and quality of their communication. Through the many rich opportunities to talk about texts, find ways to support pupils of all ages with:

1. Exploring their ideas in sophisticated ways.

2. Analysing effectively and moving away from merely regurgitating

3. Skilful cohesion of points to build strong complex ideas.

"Reading is the power that gives us energy to laugh and cry."

Summer, Year 4, Age 8

How Can We Get Children To Understand What They Are Reading?

"Reading without understanding is like swallowing food without chewing. It is during the act of chewing that all the wonderful textures and flavours are experienced."

Chapter 7

Summary

 Pupils need support to express themselves in higher order language.

 Providing cohesive words will encourage well-crafted, sentence-driven talk.

 Stamina-building reading styles should be valued alongside comprehension-driven activity.

 The 'disconnect' between certain pupils and books/authors should be explored. Why are they not engaging?

How Can We Get Children to Understand What They Are Reading?

Oliver Jeffers' book, *The Incredible Book Eating Boy*, is a fascinating tale about a young boy called Henry, who loves books:

"But not like you and I love books, no. Not quite…Henry loved eating all sorts of books. Story books, dictionaries, atlases, joke books, books of facts, even maths books….And he was going through them at a fierce rate."

This delightful tale underlines our greatest hopes for emerging readers. We want them to consume books at a 'fierce rate' and with excitement and energy. Alongside this consumption, we want them to chew books over, savour them and enjoy them. We have all taught pupils who are skilled at decoding and can plough through reams of writing almost robotically. Yet when asked a question about what they've read, they unfortunately have no clue. This is because all their energies have been directed at fluency, leaving them with no capacity to comprehend the content. On the journey to becoming 'expert readers', pupils have to work on flow, effortlessness and automaticity, so they can unlock space to think deeply about what they are reading. Once fluency is in place, the reading challenge accelerates to the next level. Pupils become consciously aware of what reading demands of their brains and how it contributes to their capacity to think, feel, infer and understand other human beings. Pupils are often fairly poor at following lines of enquiry and describing their thoughts about books. Alongside this, they may struggle to accept the personal responsibility required on their part. In the two-way relationship between the reader and the written word, the onus is on the reader to really think about the words and use personal insights to reveal meaning. These relationships, between readers and writers, can vary according to age, gender, culture and even across history. It is the changing nature of them, through time and location, which makes reading so fascinating – as we explore its meaning for us and others.

Through reading, we can help children to acquire an ever-deepening knowledge of words, their meanings and the breadth of language at their disposal to convey increasingly complex ideas. Without books, we would be devoid of: historical records, tales of ancient civilisations, a plethora of poetry, a panacea of play scripts and the gifts of humanity wrapped up in so many wonderful stories.

The language of books is vastly different from the everyday spoken word and pupils might be surprised to learn they can choose from a million English language words to convey a precise shade of meaning. Alongside text messaging and 'Snapchatting', children need to become familiar with the formality of written language: its subtle nuances and the well-considered vocabulary choices that constitute a beautiful piece of writing.

Word Count

Word Count *(www.wordcount.org)* is an interactive tool that ranks the 86,800 most frequently used English words. Each word is displayed on a visual scale, with the preceding and subsequent words offering a barometer of relevance. This online charting device serves to remind us that the more challenging, uncommon words are far less likely to be spoken in our everyday conversations. They remain the preserve of many great writers through history, yet are equally available for use by today's aspiring readers and writers.

In the following traditional excerpts, bold words have been ranked using Word Count. See the charts over page.

*"High above the city, on a tall column, stood the statue of the Happy Prince. He was **gilded** all over with thin leaves of fine gold, for eyes he had two bright sapphires, and a large red ruby glowed on his sword-hilt. He was very much admired indeed. 'He is as beautiful as a weathercock,' remarked one of the Town Councillors, who wished to gain a reputation for having artistic taste; 'only not quite so useful,' he added, fearing lest people should think him unpractical, which he really was not.*

'Why can't you be like the Happy Prince?' asked a sensible mother of her little boy, who was crying for the moon. 'The Happy Prince never dreams of crying for anything.'

'I am glad there is someone in the world who is quite happy,' muttered a disappointed man as he gazed at the wonderful statue.

The Understanding of Reading

Understanding

Retrieval

Justifications

Explanations

Summarise

Comprehension

A System for Success

THE STYLISTICs

'He looks just like an angel,' said the Charity Children as they came out of the cathedral in their bright scarlet cloaks, and their clean white pinafores.

'How do you know?' said the Mathematical Master, 'you have never seen one.'

'Ah! but we have, in our dreams,' answered the children; and the Mathematical Master frowned and looked very **severe**, for he did not approve of children dreaming.

One night there flew over the city a little Swallow. His friends had gone away to Egypt six weeks before, but he had stayed behind, for he was in love with the most beautiful Reed. He had met her early in the spring as he was flying down the river after a big yellow moth, and had been so attracted by her **slender** waist that he had stopped to talk to her."

The Happy Prince by Oscar Wilde

	Ranking on www.wordcount.org
gilded	15,997th position
severe	2,198th position
slender	8,482th position

"All the songs of the east speak of the love of the nightingale for the rose in the silent starlight night. The winged songster **serenades** the fragrant flowers. Not far from Smyrna, where the merchant drives his loaded camels, proudly arching their long necks as they journey beneath the **lofty** pines over holy ground, I saw a hedge of roses. The turtle-dove flew among the branches of the tall trees, and as the sunbeams fell upon her wings, they glistened as if they were mother-of-pearl. On the rose-bush grew a flower, more beautiful than them all, and to her the nightingale sung of his woes; but the rose remained silent, not even a dewdrop lay like a tear of sympathy on her leaves. At last, she bowed her head over a heap of stones, and said, 'Here rests the greatest singer in the world; over his tomb will I spread my fragrance, and on it I will let my leaves fall when the storm **scatters** them. He who sung of Troy became earth, and from that earth I have sprung. I, a rose from the grave of Homer, am too lofty to bloom for a nightingale.' Then the nightingale sung himself to death."

The Nightingale by Hans Christian Andersen

	Ranking on www.wordcount.org
serenades	63,652th position
lofty	15,422th position
scatters	51,709th position

Now consider the rich literary devices in these passages:

"All the songs of the east speak of the love of the nightingale for the rose in the silent starlight night."
Personification of the birdsong, appearing to 'speak of' this romance.

...ls should savour ...ks. A Year 3 ...l enjoying 'The ...edible Book Eating ... by Oliver Jeffers.

"...not even a dewdrop lay like a tear of sympathy on her leaves."
Simile for comparison underlines the rose's apparent lack of emotion.

These are perfect examples of the **unique language** of books, more likely to be acquired by pupils who are 'read to' and/or who read often themselves. Examining literary devices, such as these, is the first step towards pupils acquiring the understanding that texts contain, amongst other features:

▶ sophisticated structures
▶ multi-clause sentences
▶ poetic phrases
▶ words used figuratively (or in unusual places) to catch our attention

Professor Victoria Purcell-Gates, an internationally-recognised literacy education researcher, studied two groups of five year olds (with similar socio-economic status and parental education levels). However, one group had been 'well read to' (five times a week); the other group had not. The two groups were asked to recount a birthday, pretending to tell the story to a doll.

"The differences were unmistakable. When the children in the 'well-read-to' group told their stories, they used not only more of the special 'literary' language of books than the other children, but also more sophisticated syntactic forms in their own language. They were also better able to understand the oral and written language of others."
Cited by Maryanne Wolf in Proust & The Squid

We know that all pupils, and particularly those who are not encouraged to read at home, need support with truly comprehending what they are reading. The ability to delve deeper, going below the surface of a text, can be yielded from a highly-focused approach with the *Reading Rainbow*. Comprehension skills blossom as pupils are guided in a structured way, learning to unpeel the layers of meaning in words, phrases and sentences. Going beyond the surface layers of reading is critical for equipping readers with the strategies, pathways and tools needed to synthesise an author's ideas and form their own personal opinions.

The understanding of reading: STYLISTIC sentence starters

Pupils need structures that enable them to engage in extensive and critical dialogues about books. Guidance is particularly necessary around skills such as: discussing the setting, commenting on textual structure, investigating relationships, identifying key themes and considering whether authors achieved their intended impact. Extracting meaning from texts is not easy and pupils' thinking can be fashioned and moulded into clearer constructions using these sentence starters as frameworks.

Outlined **on the following pages** is an extensive range of Key Stage 1 and 2 sentence starters that explore each lens in detail. These talking frames promote deep, targeted thinking and enable pupils to realise that what has been learnt in one text can be applied to their analysis of others. The sense of interrelatedness inspired by the *Reading Rainbow* enables pupils to make meaningful comparisons.

It is through the lenses on this arch that pupils discover their connectivity with books/texts. For teachers, these discussion areas will quickly highlight pupils who are/ aren't properly engaged with the material. Where pupils are disconnected, some of the factors might include:

1. The text is too difficult and unknown words impede understanding.
2. The plot line is not intriguing enough, or the reader is having difficulties empathising or relating to the main protagonist.
3. The material (non-fiction) is in a subject area the reader has no interest in.
4. Confusion has occurred and the author hasn't resolved this quickly enough to curb the reader's frustration. This often happens in the first three chapters of a book, when deceits/ambiguities are laid down to be resolved later.

Year 5 pupils exploring the popularity of the word 'skittishly', which featured on the 2016 reading SAT.

Key Stage 2 pupils are able to articulate their ideas more formally using these sentence structures.

KS1 STYLISTICs:

Setting

The setting of the story is …

So far, we have learned the place is _____ and the time is _____.

The author tells us about the setting when …

The illustrations reveal more about the setting because …

The setting changes as the story unfolds because …

A descriptive sentence for the setting was: …

The setting for this non-fiction text is in the past/present/future …

The different settings explained in this non-fiction text are: …

Text Layout/Structure

The words are in bold because …

Words are in italics because …

Paragraphs help organise the writing …

The sentence/word _____ stands on its own so that …

The front cover tells us …

Headings and subheadings are used to …

The pictures/diagrams add …

Chapter headings make the reader …

Yes/No Relationships

The characters who are friends are ...

The characters who are enemies are ...

_____(insert character name) secretly/openly feels ...

This character connects with ...

Problems occur in the relationship when ...

He/She acts like a mother/father when ...

Their relationship is rewarding because ...

The relationship is believable because ...

 Logical Meaning-Making

The sequence of the story so far is ...

The big ideas in this text are ...

I am unsure what happens ...

The outline of the story is: ...

I would summarise the bare bones of the story as: ...

The main points are ...

I predict that ...

The key parts of this text are: ...

Interrogating Facts/Opinions

I have found three facts. They are ...

The facts outlined are ...

Opinions are confused with facts ...

The author's opinion is ...

The character's opinion is ...

The character does not know all the facts ...

_____ is evidence of an opinion.

If I reviewed this book, I would say ...

Solving Problems

The problem in the story is ...

The problem the main character has ...

The problem occurs when ...

The solution is ...

The characters who help solve the problem are ...

The problem was predictable/unexpected because ...

The problem was big/small because ...

I have experienced the same problem when ...

Themes

The themes in this story are ...

The themes are common because ...

The themes are unusual ...

Other stories with a similar theme(s) are: ...

The theme is clear because ...

The theme is muddled because ...

The author drives this theme by ...

A popular theme is ...

 Impact

We feel that the impact of the book ...

This book impacts on my feelings about ...

The author has tried to impact the reader by ...

The impact of this part of the story is ...

The author had a strong/weak impact on ...

The most powerful part of this story was ...

The impact of this non-fiction book is ...

The layout of this non-fiction text makes certain aspects 'stand out'. For example, ...

Characters

The central character is ...

A low/high point for the character is ...

I liked/didn't like the main character because ...

The hero is ...

The villain is ...

The author develops the character by ...

The character changes when ...

This action reveals that the character's personality is ...

KS2 STYLISTICs:

 Setting

The backdrop to this story is ...

The time period of this story is ...

The majority of the action in this story takes place in ...

The author creates a believable setting by ...

Description used by the author to set the scene evokes ...

The setting contributes to the mood of the story by ...

The era explored in this non-fiction book is ...

Setting is critical in this non-fiction book because ...

Text Layout/Structure

The author finishes the chapter on ...

The front cover entices readers by ...

The author's chapter titles are ...

The blurb on the back cover is effective/ineffective because ...

Some interesting layout features are: ...

The most striking aspect of this book's layout is ...

Information in this non-fiction book is made eye-catching by ...

A small and interesting layout feature is ...

 Yes/No Relationships

Negative relationships in the story are ...

Positive relationships in the story are ...

The central character fosters interesting relationships by ...

The relationship between _____ and _____ is unbelievable/realistic because ...

The emotions between the two characters ...

We can relate to the relationship between ...

The central character's decision to _____ changes ...

Relationships are explored in this non-fiction book when ...

Logical Meaning-Making

As a reader, I was clear about _____ but confused by ...

In summary, the chronological order of events is: ...

The key ideas in this story are: ...

The author focuses on different aspects in varying detail. One part ...

There are/aren't any time shifts in this story but ...

The sequence of the plot reveals ...

The main aspects explored in this non-fiction text are: ...

This non-fiction text can/cannot be read out of sequence because ...

Interrogating Facts/Opinions

The central character is certain of ...

We know the same/more/less facts than the central character ...

The central character's opinion is ...

The author's viewpoint is revealed when ...

A fact in this story is _____ but an opinion is ...

Facts are disclosed in this story by ...

Some of the most interesting facts in this non-fiction book are: ...

In my opinion, this text is a poor/good read because ...

Solving Problems

The main character's problem is small/large because ...

We expected/didn't expect the main character to solve the problem by ...

We are/are not sympathetic to the main character's problem because ...

Conflict is created in this story ...

Unfortunately, the main character causes his/her own problems by ...

There is a satisfactory/unsatisfactory resolution to the problem ...

The central character shows poor/good resilience when ...

This non-fiction text illuminates a problem with ...

Themes

The theme that is stranded through this text is ...

The _____ theme is most notably demonstrated by ...

Overall, we believe the theme in this book can be captured as ...

The theme could be _____ or _____ because ...

The true meaning of the story is revealed when ...

The theme is _____ and other stories with this theme are ...

Ultimately, the theme is crystallised for the reader when ...

In this non-fiction book, there is a theme borne out by the author's voice about ...

Impact

The writer's intended impact at this point is ...

As a reader, the impact is ...

By choosing the language _____, the impact is ...

When the main character _____, the impact on the reader is ...

A huge impact on our impression of the central character occurs when ...

The section _____ does little to impact on/change the reader's point of view about ...

The impact of this non-fiction book is ...

Particular design and layout features have the impact of ...

Characters

The main character is well developed/underdeveloped by the author because ...

The protagonist in this story represents ...

The main character's personality can be summed up as: ...

Some of the 'highs' experienced by the main character are: ...

Some of the 'lows' experienced by the main character are: ...

The central character is/is not a typical hero/heroine because ...

The significant people in this non-fiction text are: ...

Experts' direct quotes are used in this non-fiction text to ...

Themes

choose · similar · point · obvious · subject · glean · life · select · idea · combine

- The themes in this story are ...
- The themes are common because ...
- The themes are unusual ...
- Other stories with a similar theme(s) are: ...
- The theme is clear because ...
- The theme is muddled because ...
- The author drives this theme by ...
- A popular theme is ...

Characters

hero · personality · change · motive · heroine · learns · positive · journey · main · negative

- The central character is ...
- A low/high point for the character is ...
- I liked/didn't like the main character because ...
- The hero is ...
- The villain is ...
- The author develops the character by ...
- The character changes when ...
- This action reveals that the character's personality is ...

Impact

strikes · communicated · effect · employs · experience · intended · depth · interrelated · generate · elaborate

- The writer's intended impact at this point is ...
- As a reader, the impact is ...
- By choosing the language _____ the impact is ...
- When the main character _____ the impact on the reader is ...
- A huge impact on our impression of the central character occurs when ...
- The section _____ does little to impact on/change the reader's point of view about ...
- The impact of this non-fiction book is ...
- Particular design and layout features have the impact of ...

Setting

describe · environment · stark · believable · backdrop · scene · viewpoint · perspective · era · surroundings

- The backdrop to this story is ...
- The time period of this story is ...
- The majority of the action in this story takes place in ...
- The author creates a believable setting by ...
- Description used by the author to set the scene evokes ...
- The setting contributes to the mood of the story by ...
- The era explored in this non-fiction book is ...
- Setting is critical in this non-fiction book because ...

KS1 and KS2 Reading Thinking Kits - The STYLISTICs.
Complete resource available from www.thetrainingspace.co.uk

Consider

Organising a regular *Top Five Favourite Books* celebration from each class across the school. Compare different year groups' favourites. Explore the popularity of other titles written by these authors. The top five disappointing reads can also be shared, so pupils can begin to recognise they don't have to like everything. To develop debating skills, two pupils/groups of pupils can go 'head to head' - with one arguing that a certain book was excellent and the other taking the opposite position.

School Impact Points

Create a policy that discourages lazy commentary about books. There needs to be zero tolerance for half-hearted comments such as:

► *I liked it 'cos it had good describing words.*
► *The author showed good imagination.*
► *It was really interesting.*

Some children tend to 'get by' in classrooms, using just enough effort to survive a lesson. Weak interactions need bolstering, with a wide range of vocabulary and book-based language. Children should be challenged on their just-about-relevant comments. Schools which excel, with vibrant reading curriculums, have high expectations of 'talk'. It needs to be based on sharp, clear explanations, which extend both the individual's thinking as well as that of their peers.

Xarles, Year 4, Age 8

What Reading Competencies Do Children Need?

"If pupils' reading diets are not sufficiently varied, they will suffer from language deprivation. Flimsy offerings are no substitute for carefully-crafted, word-rich feasts, which inspire children to gorge on sentences and chomp through chapters. Children must read zealously – and most importantly – of their own volition."

Chapter 8

Summary

- [x] The ANALYTICS, on the bottom arch of the *Reading Rainbow*, are the most challenging aspects of reading comprehension for pupils.

- [x] Greater reading stamina will enhance pupils' higher order competencies, as well as developing their abilities to link, compare and contrast texts.

- [x] Reading boosts general knowledge, which in turn creates a strong bedrock of understanding that enriches pupils' relationships with other books.

- [x] Making connections between all aspects of the *Reading Rainbow* helps pupils to develop joined-up, in-depth thinking.

HOOKED ON BOOKS

What Reading Competencies Do Children Need?

Reading is paramount for developing writers, who need a close enough command of the language to exploit its subtleties and nuances. Through successful authors, children learn to craft language into precise, truthful shades of meaning (hyperbole excepted). The interplay between reading and writing, and the fact that working on one will improve the other, means they go 'hand in hand' as we work to improve standards in literacy. All teachers want avid readers, who find language engaging, gratifying and purposeful, and this is where *Book Talk* successfully delivers. It offers both a coherent philosophy and a manageable structure for developing skilled readers – with deep appreciation and understanding of language.

"Teachers who are excellent at teaching reading and writing have developed coherent principles and a systematic view towards literacy, involving substantial attention to meaning. Teachers who shape effective readers and writers are readers themselves and demonstrate that language is powerful, pleasurable and purposeful."

Medwell et al (1998); Frater (2000); Cremin et al. (2014)

Focus books are given a very warm welcome at Woodhill Primary School, Woolwich.

Reading stamina

One of the key challenges for primary teachers is building pupils' commitment to books. In order to boost reading stamina, teachers should limit the number of short extracts used for teaching. Pupils need to be acquainted with complete texts, which call for deep understanding and careful examination of the ever-changing nuances of central characters' positions. In fact, children need regular and systematic exposure to the challenging, formal structures of the written word.

Reading online (with its ease of access) makes pupils less inclined to read inferentially, analytically or critically. So how do we lure them away from the internet and towards these vital reading competencies? In my own childhood, much time and effort was invested in the acquisition of great books. After a half-hour bus journey into the centre of Birmingham, followed by a trudge across the city to the six-floor Central Library, I was certainly going to make each journey worthwhile. The place was a labyrinth of treasures and it was a joy to scour for books until one pricked my interest enough to be keenly devoured. Hour upon hour was spent drifting in and out of the pages, enjoying and soaking up the written word. I remember vividly when Prince Charles – in a 1988 BBC documentary, *A Vision of Britain* – said the 1974 *Brutalist* library, designed by John Madin, looked like:

'a place where books were incinerated, not kept'

The Competencies of Reading

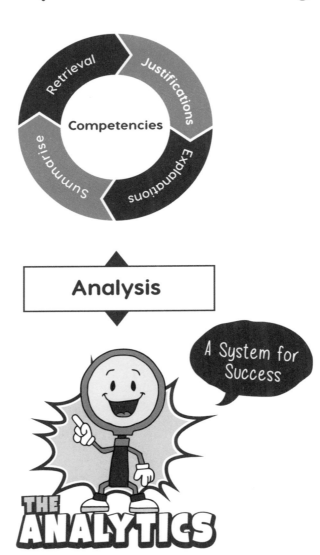

This comment personally stung as it seemed to attack more than the architecture, suggesting the resident books were not valued or cared for. Sadly, my much-loved library no longer exists: it was demolished to make way for the Birmingham Rep. For me, it was a place where books were immortalised, not destroyed, and lives on in my mind as a sanctuary. One of my favourite genres as a child was non-fiction books about significant people; in particular, women who had changed the world in some way through their actions, inventions or scientific discoveries. Today's internet-savvy pupils have access to far greater volumes of information than my generation. I use the term 'access' because this information is more likely to be 'looked at' than studied, reflected upon and absorbed. There is no doubt that today's learners have a wealth of bite-sized chunks of information available at their fingertips. However, this surely cannot compare to the quality of a well-researched, lovingly-crafted, non-fiction book, whose expert author has devoted a year* or more of their life to the project.

Knowledge

Information isn't truly *knowledge* until it's applied in context or to other experiences or situations. Knowledge comes from understanding relationships and forming conclusions, or hypotheses, through critical thinking. In reading a wide range of non-fiction texts, primary-aged children are constantly growing their knowledge banks.

*average length of time to write a book, according to *Information is Beautiful* by David McCandless.

Make your library a fun place to visit with authors and readers as special guests.

Non-fiction texts build pupils' knowledge of the world and provide insights that can all too often be left out of fiction.

These information quests are well worth encouraging, as the more children know about a time period, or a place, the more they will want to learn. With ever-growing knowledge comes a greater yield of **meaning** – through increased discoveries of new texts, as well as interconnections formed from the information gleaned.

Thinking out loud

Libraries, class bookcases and personal copies of books are precious. This preciousness is revealed through private reading; however, it is only through group discussions that the greater richness of books is exposed (as details and connections are revealed that may not have been obvious from personal reflection). To help pupils move from internal appreciation to external sharing of ideas, sentence frames can be very useful.

Classrooms that promote high-level *Book Talk* expect pupils to listen to one another as they explain their ideas. Children embrace the 'talk frame', using sentence starters to ensure there is a formality and quality to their discussions. Every session is an opportunity to embed the habits of evaluation, interpretation and debate. A *Book Talk* approach builds pupils' confidence and enables them to carry lines of enquiry that deepen understanding and reveal many interesting facets of an author's thinking/intent.

KS1 ANALYTICS:

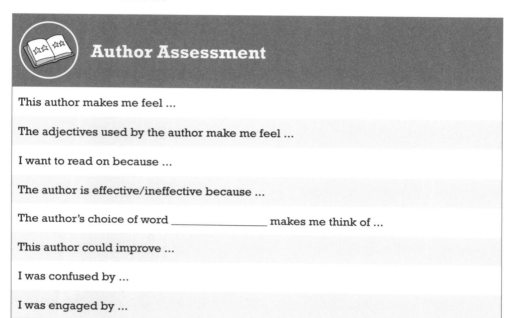

Author Assessment

This author makes me feel ...

The adjectives used by the author make me feel ...

I want to read on because ...

The author is effective/ineffective because ...

The author's choice of word _____ makes me think of ...

This author could improve ...

I was confused by ...

I was engaged by ...

Navigating Genres

This text is fiction because ...

This is a non-fiction text because ...

The story language I found was: ...

The genre features are: ...

The sentences I expected were: ...

The sentence _____ was unexpected because ...

The layout tells us ...

I know this is a _____ because ...

Accessing Phonics & Grammar

I can read ...

This is a tricky word because ...

The interesting adjectives are: ...

These verbs convey ...

A complex sentence is: ...

The writer uses ...

This word choice makes the reader ...

I can find these adverbs: ...

Language

The effective/less effective language is ...

This word is repeated to ...

This short/long sentence has an impact because ...

This description evokes ...

Poetic language is used here to ...

This image makes me think of ...

The word/sentence _____ stands out because ...

The author spends time describing _____ because ...

Your Personal Opinions

I liked/didn't like ...

The words I connected with were ...

This sentence made me feel ...

This picture/word made me think of ...

If I were the character, ...

This book tells us more about ...

If I jumped in the book, I would ...

This book was believable because ...

 Trawling for Evidence

The author uses ...

This proves that ...

We have found this evidence_____. It shows that ...

The pictures act as evidence of ...

We thought _____ was an important chunk because ...

_____ could be evidence of ...

This quote tells us ....

Our detective work has found _____ , which ...

Inferring/Deducing

This picture tells us more about ...

This word suggests ...

This sentence hints at ...

This sentence is evidence for ...

If I were _____, I would ...

This quote shows ...

The narrator is ...

I agree/disagree with ...

Considering Deeper Messages

The message is ...

The big idea is ...

The moral is ...

The most memorable part is ...

The author is trying to address ...

The hero/villain is ...

The message is powerful/effective because ...

I have read _____ that has the same message ...

Stating Predictions

My idea for what happens next is ...

If you think about what has happened already, it makes sense that ...

We predict that ...

We believe that ...

One of the possible things that might happen is ...

We foresee ...

The plot has been predictable/unpredictable so far, which means ...

We conclude that the next event ...

KS2 ANALYTICS:

 Author Assessment

If we were to review this book, we would give it _____ stars and make the comment ...

This is a _____ read because ...

Despite the good aspects of _____, the weaker parts ...

In conclusion, we would recommend/not recommend this book to a friend because ...

Overall, the book is successful/unsuccessful because ...

I would give this book _____ out of 10 based on ...

Elements of the book were predictable/unpredictable, which ...

I was engaged by ...

Navigating Genres

We know we are reading a _____ narrative because ...

The genre of our book is _____. We know this because ...

There are particular clues in the text that show us we are reading ...

Our book is closer to adventure writing than horror writing because ...
(insert relevant genre).

This book breaks/fulfils genre conventions by ...

The purpose of this book was ...

Typically, this non-fiction text ...

This non-fiction text is different from others of its type because ...

Accessing Phonics & Grammar

The syntax of this sentence creates ...

The writer makes interesting grammatical choices, particularly ...

The most arresting adjectives used by the writer are: ...

A sentence that 'caught our eye' was _____ because ...

Short sentences are used by the writer when _____, which creates ...

This long sentence _____ is effective because ...

A grammatical pattern in this non-fiction book is: ...

Some interesting grammatical choices made by the writer are: ...

Language

The most/least effective language in the text is ...

The writer uses poetic devices such as ...

Imagery is used/not used by the writer to describe the ...

Description is strong in this part of the story when ...

A juxtaposition is created by language use when ...

To engage the reader, the writer has deployed a technique ...

The language in this non-fiction text is typical/not typical of ...

The most fascinating aspect of the language used in this non-fiction piece is ...

Your Personal Opinions

We believe that this book is ...

We have found it easy/difficult to relate to this book because ...

This book does/does not reflect today's society because ...

At times, this book was challenging to read because ...

The strengths of this book are: ...

The weaknesses of this book are: ...

We believe this book is like 'real life' because ...

This is an effective/ineffective non-fiction text because ...

Trawling for Evidence

We would like to showcase this piece of evidence to explain ...

These three pieces of evidence, from different places in the text, work together to ...

We have found a small clue, which other readers might have missed, that ...

Even though it is not stated directly, this evidence _____ suggests that ...

Statement about the text: _____. The supporting evidence for this is ...

By drawing together _____ and _____, we can conclude that ...

The writer doesn't directly state _____ but hints at it through ...

This non-fiction text uses evidence such as _____ to ...

Inferring/Deducing

Hints are provided by the author about ...

These two aspects _____ and _____, when considered in tandem, suggest ...

The writer gives the reader the impression of _____ by ...

Our interpretation of this section of the story is ...

We can make a reasoned assumption that _____ because ...

We believe that the central character is _____, indicated by ...

We can infer that the writer's viewpoint on _____ is ...

We are convinced, through several references to _____, that ...

Considering Deeper Messages

This book has a helpful message about ...

The most memorable parts of the book are: ...

The moral message of this story is ...

This book reveals _____ about human nature, shown by ...

The hero/heroine of the story grows to represent ...

A deep message is explored in this book through ...

The message of this story is relevant because ...

This non-fiction text conveys a message about ...

Stating Predictions

At this stage in the story, we believe that ...

We predict that _____ and we think we are right because ...

It is easy/difficult to predict what will happen next because ...

Our previous predictions were accurate/inaccurate because ...

In line with other stories about _____, we predict ...

We can justify our prediction about ...

This non-fiction text is predictable in the following ways: ...

This non-fiction text is unpredictable in the following ways: ...

"It seems unfair that they have to leave home. It would be horrible if that happened."
Exploring empathy with a pupil.

KS1 and KS2 Reading Thinking Kits - The ANALYTICS.

Complete resource available from www.thetrainingspace.co.uk

Consider

Displaying large *Reading Rainbows* - to show pupils the range of ways in which books can be interrogated. Investigate whether or not the same lenses are being overused in some classrooms. This information will be useful to the English subject leader, who will be able to ensure that more difficult/obscure areas are tackled.

School Impact Points

① The *Reading Rainbow* helps pupils to interconnect ideas within books and across books and provides a thinking frame for all textual situations. Share the *Reading Rainbow* with pupils and encourage them to see how the layers provide rich sources for thinking.

② Ensure that *Book Talk* is well developed to promote the understanding of facts, contexts and the connections that make texts meaningful.

③ Observe pupils across a range of ages and notice how they express their understanding through the *Reading Rainbow* lenses. Discuss areas that require more direction and support, so there is a whole-school approach to ensuring successful communication across all lenses.

Alice, Year 3, Age 7

How Do You Go Beyond Book Talk?

"Book Talk supports pupils in finding their voices, taking responsibility for their group roles and fostering the development of others. It encourages them to think for themselves as well as to communally expand one another's thinking. Through listening to others' opinions, pupils also learn to structure and strengthen their own arguments."

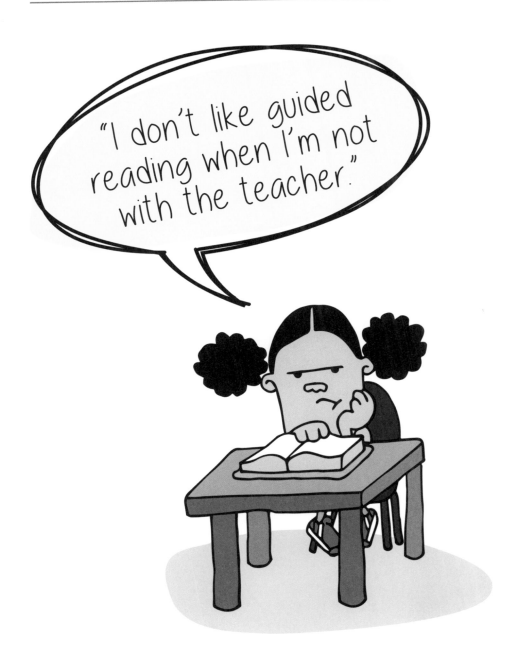

Chapter 9

Summary

 Leadership roles can really strengthen pupils' thinking during the wide and copious reading facilitated by *Book Talk*.

 These roles can start at basic levels of responsibility, increasing in status with developing expertise.

Recognition, in the form of celebratory displays, should be given to pupils whose feedback deepens others' understanding of events, moments or illustrations. This will underline your school's commitment to reading and encourage other pupils to articulate their own intriguing/ interesting thoughts.

How Do You Go Beyond Book Talk?

Book Talk can evolve into a very independent segment of the day, whereby pupils manage their own lines of questioning within their groups. Once they are really familiar with the *Reading Rainbow*, and the meanings of its component parts, they can organise their own text interrogations through any given lens. Potentially, this can also be a chance to make more written jottings about their ideas (or *Think with Ink*).

Questioning and critical analysis skills develop with practice, as do pupils' expectations about levels of difficulty and challenge. They begin to understand more closely how a teacher pushes thinking through 'pause time', appreciating the need to allow time and space for others to explain their ideas in detail. From the outset, these skills need to be modelled robustly by the class teacher – so pupils are able to replicate them within their groups.

Once teachers and pupils are familiar with the procedures of *Book Talk*, and have mastered the skills that need to be orally showcased, pupils can be allowed more autonomy to run smaller sessions tailored to their needs. To ensure coverage of all 27 lenses on the *Reading Rainbow*, it is probably best if the teacher declares the 'three reasons to read' – before allowing pupils to manage their group explorations.

Pupils with distinct roles during 'Book Talk' excel in their specialisms and are able to build skills in the areas of expertise.

Case study

I was fortunate enough to observe Year 6 teacher Sharon Green, skilfully developing this pupil autonomy to propel her class 'beyond' *Book Talk*. It showed she truly understood the art of fostering mature readers – able to both appreciate and question content. Sharon captures the process as follows:

"The children have to interrogate the text and rehearse a coherent response that includes appropriate evidence. This is whole-class reading comprehension at a deep level. They are self-motivated to develop clear, concise, evidence-based answers."

Sharon believed *Book Talk* roles had helped her pupils to:

▶ better articulate their ideas

▶ capture succinct points

▶ make comparisons between texts and authors (due to the increasing number of complete texts read).

Pupils need encouragement to launch their opinions and it can help to use the practical analogy of 'jumping into a book'. This enables them to see they have high levels of control over what they choose to zoom into and grapple with as part of the reading debate. Once children realise they are in the driving seat, it gives them the confidence to dig deeper for meanings/ layers of meaning.

Assigning roles

Leader/teacher

One pupil takes the role of *leader/teacher* – the expert who challenges answers and pushes for further detail. He/she also outlines the required sentence starters, so as to scaffold more in-depth explanation. Part and parcel of this role is to bring other group members into the conversation using questions (*e.g. Do you agree? How would you have answered that question? Is there anything to add?*) before inviting the original contributor to respond. In this role, pupils gain a deep understanding of the processes involved in building comprehensive answers. It strengthens their abilities to answer retrieval-type questions, as well as those requiring the higher order skills of inference and deduction.

Other examples of teacherly questions include: *Can you prove it? How do you know? What evidence do you have?*

BASIC LEVEL

▶ Ensures every group member reads during sessions.

▶ Organises/chooses partners for paired reading, arranging a 'three' if required.

▶ Chooses who will start the group reading.

ADVANCED LEVEL

▶ Sets required sentence starters for the group.

▶ Asks challenging and qualifying questions to extend pupils' thinking.

▶ Ensures evidence is provided, from text or illustrations, to qualify points.

Facilitator

The prime purpose of this role is to ensure inclusivity for all. When working in this mode, pupils need to be aware of fairness and parity and ensure an even distribution of chances for members to take part. Through a mix of nurturing and challenge, the *facilitator* enables all members to feel included and listened to. Direct questions are asked to pupils who have not had a chance to respond, and suggestions are made to the leader/teacher about who might need to be included in a wider debate. The *facilitator* also has responsibility for extending thinking through comments/questions, so that debates are rich and lively.

Examples of qualifying questions include: *Can you add more detail to that? Why do you think that? Can you explain that further?*

The *facilitator* can also encourage pupils to respond to their peers' ideas – either showing agreement or offering an alternative idea with supporting evidence.

Pupil Roles During Book Talk

Book Talk Leader

- Makes sure all of the group reads during a session.
- Decides partners for paired reading.
- Chooses who will start reading when reading as a group.

Facilitator

- Keeps the group on task.
- Makes sure that all group members are able to participate.

Gopher

- Collects any equipment needed by the group.
- Returns all equipment when session is completed.

Lexicographer

- Uses a dictionary to check the meanings of unfamiliar vocabulary.

DICTIONARY

Reporter

- Shares the group's findings with the rest of the class.

Recorder

- Records the group's findings.

BASIC LEVEL

▶ Keeps the group on task and reading with expression.

▶ Makes sure participation is high from all group members.

ADVANCED LEVEL

▶ Supports team members in grouping smaller ideas to make clearer, big ideas.

▶ Ensures all members understand concepts being discussed and extracts further ideas to substantiate points.

▶ Evaluates contributions and provides encouragement and advice to team members on how they might strengthen them.

Lexicographer

The *lexicographer* is an avid listener – alert to words that might have been read but not understood. It is his/her responsibility to check everyone is reading for meaning and that there are no gaps in understanding. Part of this role is to 'look up' unfamiliar words to establish clear definitions. Once a meaning is established, the *lexicographer* supports pupils with applying it in context. The sentence is re-read for clarity.

BASIC LEVEL

▶ Uses a dictionary to check meanings of unfamiliar words.

ADVANCED LEVEL

▶ Signals to the group when a difficult

A lexicographer is a useful asset to a 'Book Talk' group as they can use a dictionary to shed light on difficult words.

word has been read and checks everyone understands.

▶ Facilitates discussions and pools suggestions about a word's potential meaning before it is checked.

▶ Uses two pathways to search for definitions, e.g. a printed dictionary, an online publication.

▶ Recognises knowledge gaps that might need additional research, e.g. a non-fiction text might assume a level of background knowledge about an historical era. Here, the lexicographer might find broader explanations to assist the group.

Gopher

The responsibilities of the *gopher* are to ensure the group uses time effectively, has the right equipment and that each pupil has a personal copy of the same book. Sharing books is not conducive to promoting good reading habits. Individuals want to feel a personal connection to their book and to position it for comfort. Also, if individual reading is required, pupils need to be able to read at their own pace.

BASIC LEVEL

▶ Collects any equipment required by the group.

▶ Returns all equipment after sessions.

ADVANCED LEVEL

▶ Issues advice to group members about looking after equipment, e.g. Don't fold the pages of the book: use a sticky note instead.

▶ Bookmarks the sets of books so there is an agreement next time about where to pick up the text.

Reporter

The *reporter* treats all opinions and positions with respect. The group doesn't need to reach complete agreement/consensus but to explore a range of ideas and considerations. It is the *reporter's* job to reflect all opinions and represent counter-positions if relevant. All points of view should be captured and summarised, with supporting evidence.

BASIC LEVEL

▶ Synthesises the group's key ideas.

▶ Shares findings with the rest of the class.

ADVANCED LEVEL

▶ Keeps issues open for further discussion and consideration.

▶ Actively responds to other participants' ideas.

▶ Contributes/clarifies ideas so that reporting back is inclusive and reflects all viewpoints.

Pupils drawing comparisons between two texts, analysing similarities and differences.

Recorder

The *recorder* needs to accurately jot down early ideas, as well as more crystallised thoughts. Notes should summarise team discussions and decisions. These jottings should be legible enough for presentation by the reporter.

BASIC LEVEL

▶ Records the group's findings.

ADVANCED LEVEL

▶ Records the most relevant responses to frame the discussion.

▶ Asks questions to encourage sharply-focused contributions.

▶ Encourages pupils to notice patterns/themes that can tracked across a text.

▶ Makes accurate jottings, summarising key ideas and opinions.

Deepening the Moment: showcasing autonomous personal ideas

Reading analysis is most effective when there is an unambiguous focus, so discussions at any point will be more fruitful when using a specific lens. More able pupils can signal to the teacher and peers that they are **Deepening the Moment** – a mature and sophisticated level of investigation/analysis that demonstrates ownership of the process of exploring and evaluating texts. **Deepening the Moment** is challenging for pupils because it requires both clarity of thought and the self-confidence to believe a suggestion is worthy of sharing.

One teacher recently shared with me that a pupil had compared the structure of Patrick Ness' novel, *The Monster Calls* to Dickens'

A Christmas Carol. The pupil had noticed that both novels included uninvited visitors (in the form of nightmares) to present three stories the protagonist didn't want to hear, or see the relevance of, until the very end. This level of mastery and maturity shows a pupil becoming critically aware as a reader – identifying themes and conventions across stories and drawing conclusions about shapes and features used by authors. This is an excellent example of **Deepening the Moment** – a comment that enriches everyone's understanding of a text.

Group roles and responsibilities enhance pupils' maturity.

Consider

Trialling *Book Talk* roles in Key Stage 2 classrooms and monitoring pupil engagement. Ensure role types are rotated, so different children experience sessions in different capacities. Obtain - and act on - feedback from children about their favourite roles and how they could be developed further.

School Impact Points

Set up a Key Stage **Deepening the Moment** display board that celebrates pupils' oral contributions that:

▶ stretch communal thinking about a text

▶ extend others' understanding

▶ put another perspective on things

High praise needs to be given to pupils who have thought closely about their contributions and, in turn, are able to model for others how to talk in detailed, inspiring ways about texts. Here are some of my favourite **Deepening the Moment** contributions, gathered on my travels around UK schools:

"If Goldilocks had said 'sorry' instead of running away, we could have had a 'happily ever after'."
Aaron (Year 2)

"The harshness of the never-ending winter is captured in the line 'Always winter but never Christmas' that reminds us that the witch will always be evil without any of the joy of the season."
Nimrat (Year 5) on The Lion, The Witch and The Wardrobe by C.S. Lewis

"I can't see the point of that ending. It isn't that funny and takes away from the scariness of the rest of the plot that is so hard-hitting. Plus, it is based on a well-known, rubbish joke...it isn't effective."
Emily (Year 4) expressing her disappointment at Neil Gaiman's ending for Wolves in the Walls.

"I think David Walliams is disrespectful to the NHS in the opening of *The Midnight Gang.* He makes the nurses sound uncaring and the hospital sound horrible. I don't think this is true. I should know: I've been in hospital."
Oscar (Year 3)

Lola, Year 2, Age 6

How Can We Assess Reading?

"Children read to make sense of their world. We assess their reading to make sense of the meaning they discover."

Chapter 10
Summary

☑ Accurate assessment of reading ability is very difficult. Challenged by time pressures, teachers need to make 'real time' judgements across the breadth of reading abilities in a class.

☑ Reading aloud does not provide a complete picture of a pupil's reading ability.

☑ There are five developmental stages as pupils move from pre-reader to expert reader: phonological, orthographic, semantic, syntactic and morphological.

☑ Assessment criteria should parallel the 'reasons for reading' so teachers can record their findings 'live' during *Book Talk* sessions.

☑ A differentiated 'I can' assessment tool, reflecting the *Reading Rainbow* for each age group, strengthens practice by providing a seamless link between teaching and assessment.

How Can We Assess Reading?

Assessment is an integral part of the learning process. Through close observations and conversations, teachers build a comprehensive picture of the progress and learning needs of each child, which ultimately leads to improved teaching and learning. As pupils are nurtured from pre-readers to expert readers, teachers need to recognise the developmental stages along the road to full competency.

"Reading never just happens. Not a word, a concept, or a social routine is wasted in the 2,000 days that prepare the very young brain to use all the developing parts that go into reading acquisition. It is all there from the start – or not – with consequences for the rest of children's reading development, and for the rest of their lives."
Maryanne Wolf

Reading relies on many developmental processes, which eventually come together – enabling children to understand both the explicit and implicit messages of written language.

The five developmental stages of reading

Phonological development

A child gradually learns to hear, segment and understand the small units of sounds that make up words. This critically affects their ability to decode whole words.

Orthographic development

Children begin to learn that their writing system represents oral language. This gives a critical foundation for all that follows. As well as learning about the visual aspects of print, such as the features of letters, they begin to recognise common letter patterns, 'sight' words in English and also how to spell all of these new words.

Semantic and pragmatic development

Understanding of word meanings, gleaned from the language and culture around them. As this develops, laborious decoding is replaced with many more 'aha' moments (as children instantly recognise and comprehend words).

Syntactic development

Awareness of grammatical forms and structures, which helps children make sense of sentences, paragraphs and stories. This also covers how events relate to one another in a text.

Morphological development

Perhaps the least studied of the systems, this involves the conventions surrounding how words are formed from smaller, meaningful roots and units of meaning (i.e. morphemes). For example, un*pack*ed.

The interplay between these areas, which strengthens over time and with practice, is the crucial bedrock for children's reading fluency and comprehension. With increasing synchronicity comes deeper understanding, not only of written language but of themselves and the world they live in.

For teachers assessing pupils' reading abilities, the complex array of aspects makes it one of their most challenging tasks. In addition, reading assessment systems have traditionally been too far removed from daily teaching provision and experiences. Often, teachers witnessed something intriguing about a pupil's reading but it didn't fit in neatly with the descriptors.

Technology can offer opportunities to extend the ways pupils read for meaning.

Assessing reading can be stressful and time-consuming. It does not always yield accurate information and we can sometimes forget to listen carefully.

Performance of Reading Tool

"I have tons and tons of sticky notes flapping about as I often don't have time to write up an accurate quote from a pupil. A jotting makes sense on Tuesday at 10 o'clock but by Friday I've forgotten what it meant. Also, I sometimes get so engrossed in their reading explanations and discussions that I forget to assess."

Mrs. L. Smith, Studfall Junior School, Corby

The assessment of reading is more difficult than the assessment of writing. Writing can be taken away from the classroom and marked in the comfort of your own home. Reading brings an enormous set of pressures, as judgements have to be made 'live' during reading activities.

Teachers have an enormous amount of aspects to consider 'in the moment'. That moment is often fleeting and/or interrupted by a new moment from another child. The information comes 'thick and fast', with great pressure to record and/or diagnose it – often leaving teachers with a sense of missed moments. In fact, teachers up and down the country will admit that if there are gaps to be found anywhere in their assessment processes, they will be in reading.

I have worked hard, in partnership with hundreds of UK teachers, to design an assessment approach – whereby what is being taught and what is being assessed neatly match. This system allows 'real time' judgements that are timely and slick and alleviates the heavy assessment burden <u>after</u> sessions. The five crucial developmental areas are synthesised with the *Reading Rainbow* to ensure the key processes are recapped regularly through a range of lenses.

This assessment tool offers a detailed breakdown of all the reading competencies and skills to be mastered by each age group and has been designed to track progress from Foundation Stage through to Year 6. A broad range of skills is organised hierarchically, from *Progressing Towards* through *On Track to Way Ahead*. As teachers work with their daily focus groups, each 'reason to read' has associated 'I can' statements, which are both age-related and differentiated.

The *Performance of Reading Tool* really helps to shape up teacher assessment, which must be based on a broad range of evidence (observing pupils at the point of reading, discussions about what they have read, oral and written interactions with texts, as well as a rich selection of their reading across a range of subjects). Evidence is easily collected during *Book Talk* sessions and consistent attainment of all the statements means schools can be certain they are providing a comprehensive and rich reading curriculum.

Teaching reading is our duty

To improve the opportunities and outcomes for every generation, reading must be valued and promoted by every school. This requires ring-fenced time that is drenched in positivity and encouragement, so as to support pupils of all abilities.

If children are to be encouraged to read for pleasure, we must ensure we are constantly reviewing the enjoyable and captivating moments of a variety of texts.

With the ever-increasing impetus to prepare children for SAT tests, we must ensure reading doesn't become burdensome and/or always geared to answering comprehension questions. This is why *Book Talk* is a very worthwhile activity – more closely reflecting authentic reading situations beyond the classroom. Once a daily half an hour is provided for *Book Talk*, assessment will become more manageable as teachers assess their focus groups according to the 'three reasons to read', using the correct age-expectation statements.

Provided in this chapter are the complete 'I can' statements for Years 1 and 4 (one example from each key stage). The complete *Performance of Reading* Tool can be ordered from The Training Space (www.thetrainingspace.co.uk). There are two formats: one is for teachers to track progress over an academic term and the other is a colourful, accessible pupil resource (emphasising personal reading targets).

Reading, and the accurate assessment of reading, are both fundamental. Children's future life opportunities depend on us, their primary school teachers, getting it right.

Early Reader

A Year 1 Reader should be aware of the common graphemes for 40+ phonemes. Phonic decoding skills are beginning to encompass some two/three syllable words with the same grapheme-phoneme correspondences (GPCs). Children of this age should also recognise common exception words, e.g. the, a, do, today, of, said, says, are, were, was (the Year 1 Vocabulary Vest from The Writing Laundry can be used as an aide-memoire for pupils). *See Appendix for Vocabulary Vest*

The early reader should also be able to:

- ☑ read aloud many GPC words, without overt sounding/ blending, as phonic knowledge is increasingly applied to unfamiliar words.

- ☑ add word endings, such as: __s, __es, __ing, __ed, __er and __est.

- ☑ read contracted words (e.g. I'm, I'll, we'll), knowing what the apostrophe represents.

- ☑ understand new word meanings and link this understanding to words already known.

- ☑ read and understand simple sentences.

- ☑ use developing awareness of words which sound wrong/nonsensical to increasingly self-correct.

A Year 1 Reader can discuss the significance of a book title and explore important events. These events can be talked about and sequenced. Inferences about what happens next can be made on the basis of patterns revealed. Increasingly, pupils of this age can:

- ☑ explain what they are reading – and draw on what they already know/background information – to enhance understanding.

- ☑ relate events in a text to personal experiences.

- ☑ consider the characteristics of key stories, fairy tales and non-fiction texts.

Cards are available at www.thetrainingspace.co.uk

Performance of Reading

Expected Standard at Year 1 – Progressing Towards

		FANTASTIC	
F	♡ Feeling	I can identify 'action' that would make me feel a certain way.	☐
A	💬 Asking	I can find key dialogue in a text.	☐
N	👀 Noticing	I can imagine the sights I would see if I 'jumped into the book'.	☐
T	✋ Touching	I can talk about items I have touched that feel similar.	☐
A1	Action	I can find slow and fast action within a story.	☐
S	Smelling	I can relate the smells in a story to my own experiences.	☐
T1	Tasting	I can understand how food can be a social event, bringing characters together.	☐
I	Imagining	I can relate to incidents in a story and imagine how they would make me feel.	☐
C	Checking	I can enjoy books with particular rhythms, repetitions and rhymes.	☐

		STYLISTIC	
S	Setting	I can identify words about a setting.	☐
T	Text Layout/Structure	I can identify the difference between photographs and illustrations in non-fiction.	☐
Y	Yes/No Relationships	I can identify positive and negative relationships in a story.	☐
L	Logical Meaning-Making	I can read rhythmically (or use phrasing) whilst maintaining track of print.	☐
I	Interrogating Facts/Opinions	I can identify and distinguish between non-fiction and fiction books.	☐
S1	Solving Problems	I can suggest possible solutions to a story problem.	☐
T1	Themes	I can talk about the meaning of a story.	☐
I1	Impact	I can make connections between a text and my personal experiences.	☐
C	Characters	I can relate what happens to characters to my personal experiences.	☐

		ANALYTICS	
A	Author Assessment	I can identify interesting illustrations or words used by an author/illustrator.	☐
N	Navigating Genres	I can understand book conventions/terminology, e.g. front cover, title, page, beginning, end, line, word, blurb.	☐
A1	Accessing Phonics & Grammar	I can read accurately, blending sounds in unfamiliar words (GPCs taught).	☐
L	Language	I can locate and point out initial/final sounds in tricky or key words.	☐
Y	Your Personal Opinions	I can relate story settings and incidents to my own experiences.	☐
T	Trawling for Evidence	I can locate and read significant parts of a text.	☐
I	Inferring/Deducing	I can use non-fiction books to answer who? what? why? where? & how? questions.	☐
C	Considering Deeper Messages	I can comment on events and ideas in stories, poems and non-fiction.	☐
S	Stating Predictions	I can predict what might happen from illustrations.	☐

Performance of Reading
Expected Standard at Year 1 – On Track

FANTASTIC

F	♡	Feeling	I can find dialogue that would make me feel a certain way.	☐
A	💬	Asking	I can read dialogue using characters' voices.	☐
N	👀	Noticing	I can notice how writers describe different environments.	☐
T	✋	Touching	I can locate specific information to answer simple questions about touch.	☐
A1		Action	I can read action scenes with the appropriate pace.	☐
S		Smelling	I can notice when a writer includes the sense of smell.	☐
T1		Tasting	I can locate a 'celebration' in a story and say if the sense of taste is included.	☐
I		Imagining	I can notice when a character has a vivid imagination.	☐
C		Checking	I can predict sounds that might occur in stories before they happen.	☐

STYLISTIC

S		Setting	I can notice how words and illustrations work together to create settings.	☐
T		Text Layout/Structure	I can explain why authors might use charts and diagrams.	☐
Y		Yes/No Relationships	I can distinguish between friends and rivals, using picture clues and words to support my answers.	☐
L		Logical Meaning-Making	I can use pictures and words to clarify meaning.	☐
I		Interrogating Facts/Opinions	I can discuss new things I have discovered from reading.	☐
S1		Solving Problems	I can begin to talk about who helps or hinders a character with their problem.	☐
T1		Themes	I can talk about the big idea in a story.	☐
I1		Impact	I can respond to a text at many different levels, e.g. how different characters experience the same event.	☐
C		Characters	I can explore good and bad events that have an impact on a character.	☐

ANALYTICS

A		Author Assessment	I can begin to talk about authors.	☐
N		Navigating Genres	I can understand how diagrams and charts work.	☐
A1		Accessing Phonics & Grammar	I can read words containing taught GPCs & endings (_s, _es, _ing, _ed, _er, _est).	☐
L		Language	I can begin to show sentence knowledge: self-correcting, substituting words that retain grammatical sense or contextual sense.	☐
Y		Your Personal Opinions	I can make choices about the books I like and explain why.	☐
T		Trawling for Evidence	I can notice interesting words and explain how these support my personal ideas/opinions.	☐
I		Inferring/Deducing	I can begin to make predictions based on textual features, e.g. 'Once upon a time', title, captions, blurb.	☐
C		Considering Deeper Messages	I can locate specific information that reflects the message of a story.	☐
S		Stating Predictions	I can predict what might happen from illustrations and text.	☐

Performance of Reading

Expected Standard at Year 1 – Way Ahead

FANTASTIC

F	Feeling	I can draw parallels between emotions in stories and those in my own life.	☐
A	Asking	I can notice the punctuation (inverted commas) that signals a character's speech.	☐
N	Noticing	I can pair together text and pictures to explain the setting of a story.	☐
T	Touching	I can compare characters in stories through how they touch objects/others.	☐
A1	Action	I can recognise that action is the events in a story and find examples.	☐
S	Smelling	I can use my understanding of setting and situation to talk about the sense of smell.	☐
T1	Tasting	I can compare stories that include foods and explain what they tell us about characters.	☐
I	Imagining	I can comment on the use of visual strategies in some books, e.g. speech bubbles and thought bubbles to build characters.	☐
C	Checking	I can point to specific words/phrases that summarise key sounds.	☐

STYLISTIC

S	Setting	I can discuss settings and reflect on my own experiences of those environments.	☐
T	Text Layout/Structure	I can recognise when an author has decided to make a word or sentence stand out.	☐
Y	Yes/No Relationships	I can discuss how a character can have different relationships with different characters.	☐
L	Logical Meaning-Making	I can talk about the main events/key points in a text.	☐
I	Interrogating Facts/Opinions	I can consider how an author feels about characters and setting.	☐
S1	Solving Problems	I can predict a story problem before it occurs, drawing on experience of other stories.	☐
T1	Themes	I can compare stories and talk about themes.	☐
I1	Impact	I can discuss similarities/differences to other books I've read.	☐
C	Characters	I can express opinions about characters.	☐

ANALYTICS

A	Author Assessment	I can recognise how authors try to engage the reader.	☐
N	Navigating Genres	I can begin to identify and distinguish between non-fiction and fiction books.	☐
A1	Accessing Phonics & Grammar	I can read words containing more than one syllable that contain taught GPCs.	☐
L	Language	I can begin to locate and read significant words and give reasons for their importance.	☐
Y	Your Personal Opinions	I can discuss what I liked/disliked about a text.	☐
T	Trawling for Evidence	I can locate tricky words and work on their meanings.	☐
I	Inferring/Deducing	I can make simple deductions.	☐
C	Considering Deeper Messages	I can compare stories with the same messages.	☐
S	Stating Predictions	I can predict what might happen from the text.	☐

Fluent Reader

A Year 4 Reader's comprehension takes precedence over the decoding of individual words; however, they still meet further exception words, noting unusual correspondences between spellings and sounds. They are able to read high frequency words, as well as those with unusual spellings, e.g. calendar, heart, naughty and perhaps (see the Year 4 Vocabulary Vest in The Writing Laundry).

*See Appendix for Vocabulary Vest

Fluent readers demonstrate both confidence and the ability to read for more sustained periods of time. They adopt a positive attitude to reading and read for a range of purposes. Pupils with good fluency are also able to:

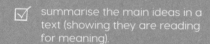 summarise the main ideas in a text (showing they are reading for meaning).

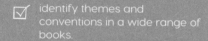 identify themes and conventions in a wide range of books.

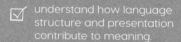 understand how language structure and presentation contribute to meaning.

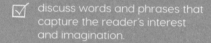 discuss words and phrases that capture the reader's interest and imagination.

An active approach is taken to finding meanings of words they do not understand (using dictionaries) and — in non-fiction texts — contents pages and indexes are used to retrieve information. The conventions of different non-fiction text types, such as biographies and non-chronological reports, are explored and the similarities/differences identified.

Performance of Reading

Expected Standard at Year 4 – Progressing Towards

FANTASTIC

F	♡	Feeling	I can appreciate that feelings are universal, regardless of the historical/social context of a story.	☐
A	💬	Asking	I can notice the effect of certain dialogue on other characters in a story.	☐
N	👀	Noticing	I can consider what a story character sees, based on the author's descriptions.	☐
T	✋	Touching	I can explore if 'touch' is more dominant in busy or quiet scenes in a narrative.	☐
A1	👊	Action	I can infer meaning from subtle character actions.	☐
S	👃	Smelling	I can select moments in a story that could be enhanced by 'smell' descriptions.	☐
T1	👅	Tasting	I can identify language used by an author that categorises 'taste' as either sweet, bitter, salty or sour.	☐
I	💭	Imagining	I can correlate character actions with their thoughts.	☐
C	👂	Checking	I can suggest sounds that could be used to further develop a narrative.	☐

STYLISTIC

S		Setting	I can consider shifts in setting and the impact on characters.	☐
T		Text Layout/Structure	I understand how 'cliffhanger' sentences, at the ends of paragraphs/chapters, encourage people to read on.	☐
Y		Yes/No Relationships	I can notice actual points in a story that reinforce or break relationships.	☐
L		Logical Meaning-Making	I can skim read to gain an overall impression of a text.	☐
I		Interrogating Facts/Opinions	I can explain new facts that I didn't know prior to reading a book.	☐
S1		Solving Problems	I can discuss many alternative solutions to a problem and debate the possible advice that other characters might give.	☐
T1		Themes	I can begin to notice that a story's theme can reveal an author's opinion about an issue.	☐
I1		Impact	I can evaluate high impact aspects of a story/non-fiction text.	☐
C		Characters	I can discuss characters and explore their motivations.	☐

ANALYTICS

A		Author Assessment	I can understand language used by authors to create imaginary worlds.	☐
N		Navigating Genres	I can evaluate different text-types and discuss their effectiveness as examples of the genre.	☐
A1		Accessing Phonics & Grammar	I can apply knowledge of prefixes and suffixes when reading.	☐
L		Language	I can identify how repetitive language can be used for effect.	☐
Y		Your Personal Opinions	I can begin to use my experience of reading to draw out similarities and differences between books.	☐
T		Trawling for Evidence	I can extract information from a non-fiction text and assess it for relevance to its intended purpose.	☐
I		Inferring/Deducing	I can draw conclusions about a story using two or more points of reference in the text.	☐
C		Considering Deeper Messages	I can notice that big messages for readers can change as plots unravel.	☐
S		Stating Predictions	I can predict what might happen from implied details (including illustrations).	☐

Performance of Reading

Expected Standard at Year 4 – On Track

FANTASTIC

F	Feeling	I can collect a range of evidence to reflect on a character's emotional responses to certain situations.	
A	Asking	I can assess the effectiveness of alternatives to the word 'said'.	
N	Noticing	I can understand that authors use detailed descriptions to enable readers to build vivid mental pictures.	
T	Touching	I can decide whether the main characters are 'tactile' through key action scenes.	
A1	Action	I can understand the two types of 'action' in stories - major events and common actions.	
S	Smelling	I can explain how the sense of smell is used to reflect social, historical and cultural traditions.	
T1	Tasting	I can identify why 'taste' is important in particular non-fiction texts.	
I	Imagining	I can understand that some characters are secretive about their real thoughts.	
C	Checking	I can explore alternative sounds that could be included in a narrative to achieve differing outcomes.	

STYLISTIC

S	Setting	I can analyse the effectiveness of settings to certain parts of stories.	
T	Text Layout/Structure	I can understand that layout choices by the author are deliberate, explaining why I believe certain decisions were made.	
Y	Yes/No Relationships	I can discuss how a relationship evolves from the beginning of a book to the end.	
L	Logical Meaning-Making	I can compare two texts and explain the similarities and differences.	
I	Interrogating Facts/Opinions	I can sort facts into most/least significant in both stories and non-fiction.	
S1	Solving Problems	I can identify the central problem of a story and how it is solved.	
T1	Themes	I can talk about the central theme of a text and summarise it, e.g. betrayal of loved ones.	
I1	Impact	I can analyse the effect of certain plot points on the reader.	
C	Characters	I can recognise how characters are presented in different ways, using text references to justify my responses.	

ANALYTICS

A	Author Assessment	I can comment on the success of texts in provoking particular responses.	
N	Navigating Genres	I can identify vocabulary and symbolic features related to text-types.	
A1	Accessing Phonics & Grammar	I can decode unknown words from roots and spelling patterns.	
L	Language	I can notice that non-fiction writers use key words for cohesion.	
Y	Your Personal Opinions	I can talk with friends about books in an opinionated and extended way, i.e. four or five sentences orally.	
T	Trawling for Evidence	I can locate information confidently, using ICT resources and skills such as text marking.	
I	Inferring/Deducing	I can infer meaning from a text, applying my knowledge of the world.	
C	Considering Deeper Messages	I can recognise that different characters can represent different messages for readers.	
S	Stating Predictions	I can predict what might happen from some implied details (including illustrations).	

Performance of Reading

Expected Standard at Year 4 – Way Ahead

FANTASTIC

F	Feeling	I can draw out evidence of dialogue or action that implies a character's feelings.	☐
A	Asking	I can discuss how opposing dialogue can create contrast in both narrative and non-fiction writing.	☐
N	Noticing	I can identify poetic devices used by the author (e.g. imagery) to create pictures for the reader.	☐
T	Touching	I can identify moments in a story when 'touch' references enhance the reader's experience.	☐
A1	Action	I can analyse the actions of a character and discuss what they reveal about personality.	☐
S	Smelling	I can infer a writer's intent through references to 'smell' at certain points in a story.	☐
T1	Tasting	I can retrieve examples of the sense of 'taste' and deduce how they create particular effects.	☐
I	Imagining	I can empathise with a central character who does not reveal their true inner thinking.	☐
C	Checking	I can locate onomatopoeic words/phrases and discuss their impact on the reader.	☐

STYLISTIC

S	Setting	I can consider the time frames of a story/non-fiction text, e.g. minute by minute, months.	☐
T	Text Layout/Structure	I can suggest layout improvements to enhance a text.	☐
Y	Yes/No Relationships	I can identify smaller relationships in a story but still explain their significance.	☐
L	Logical Meaning-Making	I can understand the thread of a whole text.	☐
I	Interrogating Facts/Opinions	I can distinguish between fact, fiction, author's opinion and personal response.	☐
S1	Solving Problems	I can reflect on the central character's success in being able to solve a problem.	☐
T1	Themes	I can understand that themes are often implied and will require supporting evidence from the text.	☐
I1	Impact	I can summarise the overall impact of a story/text on the reader.	☐
C	Characters	I can make predictions about a character's actions.	☐

ANALYTICS

A	Author Assessment	I can identify positive and negative aspects of an author's work.	☐
N	Navigating Genres	I can navigate texts quickly to locate specific information, making effective use of the contents, sections and headings.	☐
A1	Accessing Phonics & Grammar	I can read further exception words, noting unusual correspondences.	☐
L	Language	I can understand that figurative language, e.g. similes, personification, creates images.	☐
Y	Your Personal Opinions	I can discuss in detail my personal responses to books that I would/would not recommend.	☐
T	Trawling for Evidence	I can identify complex sentences and how they reveal extra information to the reader.	☐
I	Inferring/Deducing	I can explore alternatives that could have occurred in texts and assess their authenticity.	☐
C	Considering Deeper Messages	I can relate to a text and how it provides a commentary on our society today.	☐
S	Stating Predictions	I can plausibly predict what might happen from details implied and stated (including Illustrations).	☐

Consider

Designing easy-to-manage *Book Talk* records, so assessments can be made 'live' with daily focus groups. Over a week, if daily *Book Talk* sessions have occurred, you will have comprehensive assessment data for the whole class (based on the principle of five attainment groups per class).

School Impact Points

Before launching *Book Talk* in your school, take a litmus test of current attitudes and levels of engagement for reading.

Use some of the questions outlined in *Getting them Reading Early (Ofsted)* to benchmark softer data/information. Banks of questions can be found here to ask different pupil samples, from low to high attainers.

Review attitudes to reading after a strong launch of a 'We love reading' culture and regular, lively *Book Talk* sessions. Compare shifts in pupils' perceptions.

Key Stage 1 ⟶

- ▶ Do you read to someone in school?

- ▶ How often?

- ▶ Do you read with someone at home?

- ▶ Do you have a reading record/diary?

- ▶ Please may I see it? [Check how often an adult listens to the child read? Which adults? Parent/teacher/teaching assistant?]

- ▶ Do you like this book? Why?

- ▶ What are your favourite (sorts of) books?

- ▶ What books has your teacher read to the class that you enjoyed?

- ▶ Do you feel you are a good reader? What's easy? What's difficult? How do you think you could get even better as a reader?

- ▶ Do you enjoy reading?

Key Stage 2

- ▶ Do you enjoy reading?

- ▶ Does the school have the sorts of books that you would like to read? If not, what sorts would you like more of?

- ▶ How do you find out about new books or authors that you might want to read?

- ▶ How well do you think you're getting on as a reader?

- ▶ What do you think would improve your reading even more?

- ▶ What advice does your teacher give you about your reading?

- ▶ Does anyone check what books you are reading? Do you get help/advice with what sorts of books to read?

- ▶ How many books have you read on your own this term/since you have been in this class?

- ▶ Do you read every day: at school? at home? If not, why not?

Ayush, Year 5, Age 9

Appendix

Resources to support a 'Hooked on Books' approach

A printable certificate to send to your adopted author:

Adopt an Author

Terms and Conditions

If we adopt you, then it is supposed to be a positive relationship that you enjoy and doesn't cause you stress. It might be a little bit of commitment... really little. As a class, we can tell you all about ourselves - who is the cheekiest, who is the best at poetry, who tells the worst jokes and who would like to write books when they are older.

Letters

We will write letters to you twice a year. We love making contact with our favourite authors and you can find out all about us.

Inside Stuff

We will ask nosey questions, such as: Do you have a cat? What is its name? What are your hobbies? Do you like avocados?

What's in it for you?

Book Club

We would love it if you could join us and read (at the same time) our class book and then we could share our responses and reviews.

1. A Christmas card.
2. A birthday card.
3. Advice for drafts of your writing.
4. A ready-made audience of 30 children to test out your new material.
5. A photograph of us and our favourite bits of your books.

While we would like to adopt you, in many ways you adopt us. We will send you stuff in the post. We will also send drawings of you and generally be attention-seeking. Please sign below to show us that you would like us to love you more than other authors.

Please sign here..

Celebrating Reading

A handy year planner for ensuring pupils are engaged
with many exciting reading activities.

January

Whitbread Book Award
www.goodreads.com/award/show/111-whitbread-award

February

National Storytelling Week
www.sfs.org.uk

March

World Book Day
www.worldbookday.com

World Storytelling Day
www.getstoried.com

April

International Children's Book Day
www.ibby.org

May

National Share a Story Month
www.fcbg.org.uk

June

Volunteers Week
www.volunteersweek.org.uk

Kids' Clubs Week
www.4children.org.uk

The Orange Prize
www.goodreads.com/award/show/90-orange-prize

July/August

National Summer Reading Challenge in Libraries
www.readingagency.org.uk

**The CILIP Carnegie and Kate Greenaway
Children's Book Awards**
www.carnegiegreenaway.org.uk

Respect Poetry Slam Final
www.poetrysociety.org.uk/education/

A Year View

September

International Literacy Day
www.literacyworldwide.org

October

International Poetry Challenge Day
www.writersdigest.com

National Children's Book Week
www.booktrust.org.uk

National Schools' Film Week
www.filmeducation.org

National Poetry Day
www.poetrysociety.org.uk

Family Learning Week
www.campaign-for-learning.org.uk

International School Library Day
www.iasl-slo.org

Black History Month
www.black-history-month.co.uk

The Man Booker Prize
www.bookerprize.co.uk

November

The Guardian Children's Fiction Prize
www.theguardian.com/books/guardianchildrensfictionprize

The Blue Peter Book Awards
www.booktrust.org.uk/prizes/2

December

Relax and cuddle up with a really good book.

Every Minute Counts

Child 'A' reads
1 minute each day

**180 minutes in a
school year**

8,000 words

Child 'B' reads
5 minutes each
day

**900 minutes in a
school year**

282,000 words

Child 'C' reads
20 minutes each
day

**3,600 minutes in a
school year**

1,800,000 words

Writing Laundry Year 1 - Vocabulary Vest

The full Writing Laundry - and many other useful teacher resources - are available from The Training Space (www.thetrainingspace.co.uk).

Writing Laundry Year 4 - Vocabulary Vest

arrive
answer
actually
breathe
eighth business
exercise bicycle
forwards earth
history famous
interest fruit
notice heart
particular knowledge
probably mention
potatoes occasionally
strange position
suppose purpose
through question
weight special
surprise

circle
consider
caught
decide
different
disappear
experiment
group
February
important
guide
length
material
natural
opposite
reign
sentence
although
women

YR4

Vocabulary Vest

© Jane Considine

You can download this free blank grid from our website (www.thetrainingspace.co.uk).
See over the page for an example of a pupil's jottings.

The Book Talk Jotter
Think With Ink

	ANALYTICS	STYLISTICS	FANTASTICS
MONDAY			
TUESDAY			
WEDNESDAY			
THURSDAY			
FRIDAY			

The Book Talk Jotter
Think with Ink

	FANTASTICS	SYFANTICS	AUTHENTICS
MONDAY	Before you read this book, what questions would you like to know about the topic of your book? Record questions on post it notes	I think the layout of the text is ..... Pictures, paragraphs, non-chronological order, fun facts. It has ...... If I could improve the layout I would add .... different ..... because it .... e.g page DO	The key features in this text are They help the reader by An example of this is
TUESDAY	How old is Hinduism? How old Who were the first Hindus? Hinduism? What is the population of Hindus? How many Hindus live in England?	The facts in this text are .... when it talks about .... because this is a fact because .... I know this a fact because .... An example of this is .... on page 86 au it says '....'	The vocabulary and features that are related to this type of text are ... Index, Title, sub-headings, contents, paragraphs, facts, captions and pictures this is because ..... in every non-fiction book you need to find ... good voc and pea you can half make the book more .....
WEDNESDAY	The language used in this text is .... description golden language? questions and This is because ..... every book needs good language to make it interesting An example of this is ... on page 66 it says what it says	The layout of this text is non-chrono, paragraphs, picture, contents facts and tex box The organisational features that have been used are .. Contence, Index, page numbers and paragraphs. These are used because .. the more it the EG eg 86 ... But some understandable	The similarities are ... they both got pics, paragraphs, titles, sub-titles and page numbers 50 each The differences are that the one of then is real and the other is not this I preger to read one because ..... it is more interesting and exciting
THURSDAY	I/we would like to find out about ..... why # 15 50 because it don't tell us in the book and it m has made us curious If this book does not answer this question I could look on google or My person or the library	The least significant facts are .. How it turns blue and how putha died. I know this because on page 16, it says how k turned blue and How Pulma died An example of this is on psy 16 is says	My opinion is that this non-fiction book is about H. It very makes L about r and B interesting. I think that the PE were L about
FRIDAY	The topic related words in this text are ... Hinduism worship, God, Holy, Fesivals and beliefs life. An example is on .... the con bance whge it says into - Holy books These enhance the text by .. helpin you know	This text is about .. Hindusim, Angel and hulu life An example of this is on the contea? into index .... he added thought about explisation - off he made it very intresting	From reading this text I have learnt that this book tells you every thing about Hindus that we want to learn. It also asked all our question like who were the first Hindus? eg of this PGE 6

Book Talk Plan

Steps to Success

1. Listen: To your friends, talk about books.

2. Read: Like a teacher, clear with expression

3. Talk: Using evidence from the text.

Three Reasons to Read

FANTASTIC	STYLISTIC	ANALYTICS

Feelings	Yes/No Relationships	Stating Predictions
Sentence Starter	**Sentence Starter**	**Sentence Starter**
The most dominant emotion is...	The main character is friends/enemies with...	I predict what will happen next is...
Key Words	**Key Words**	**Key Words**
scared, happy, excited, shocked, nervous	friends, enemies, like, dislike, family	after, later, because, clues, earlier

Book Talk Plan

Steps to Success

1. Listen: To your friends, talk about books.

2. Read: Like a teacher, clear with expression.

3. Talk: Using evidence from the text.

Three Reasons to Read

FANTASTIC	STYLISTIC	ANALYTICS

Asking	Impact	Language

Sentence Starter	Sentence Starter	Sentence Starter
The most significant piece of dialogue is...	I would give my author ? out of 10 because...	The most powerful sentence so far is...

Key Words	Key Words	Key Words
impact, successful, effective, fails, unsuccessful	revealing, intent, effect, strong, weak	suggests, cleverly, focus, attention, choice

Book Talk Plan

Steps to Success

1. **Listen:** To your friends, talk about books.

2. **Read:** Like a teacher, clear with expression.

3. **Talk:** Using evidence from the text.

Three Reasons to Read

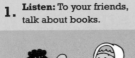

FANTASTIC

Action

Sentence Starter

A significant action by the central character is...

Key Words

impact, pace, activity, engages, propels

STYLISTIC

Characters

Sentence Starter

The main character is friends/enemies with...

Key Words

friends, enemies, like, dislike, family

ANALYTICS

Considering Deeper Messages

Sentence Starter

The moral of the story is...

Key Words

advises, learn, illustrates, teaches, moral

Book Talk Plan

Steps to Success

1. **Listen:** To your friends, talk about books.

2. **Read:** Like a teacher, clear with expression.

3. **Talk:** Using evidence from the text.

Three Reasons to Read

FANTASTIC

Feelings

Sentence Starter

A less obvious emotion is...

Key Words

intrigued, exciting, anxious, fascinating, curious

STYLISTIC

Interrogating Facts/ Opinions

Sentence Starter

I have found '_____' facts in this text

Key Words

facts, opinions, persuasive, information

ANALYTICS

Navigating Genres

Sentence Starter

I know I am reading '_____' because...

Key Words

style, language, information, question, features

Book Talk Policy

'Book Talk' is a systematic way to teach reading strategies across the whole school from Year 1 to Year 6. It is underpinned by certain guiding principles, which are outlined below:

1. Pupils are organised into reading attainment groups and share a set of the 'same' books pitched at their level with appropriate challenge.
2. All pupils in the classroom will be accessing narrative, non-fiction or poetry at the same time.
3. Pupils will partake in a daily 30 minute 'Book Talk' session and once a week will intensively work with the class teacher for a 'guided read'.
4. Sessions are themed around open-ended whole-class questions to tackle the three layers of the *Reading Rainbow*.
   "On average, reading comprehension approaches improve learning by an additional five months' progress." Education Endowment Foundation
   The use of techniques such as graphic organisers and drawing pupils' attention to text structures are likely to be particulary useful when reading a range of non-fiction texts.

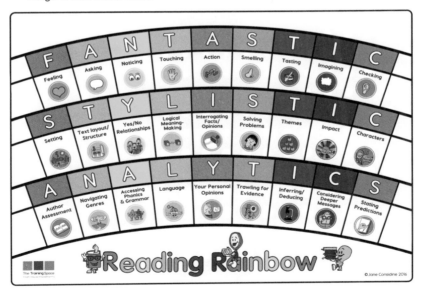

5. A hallmark of sessions is developing reading for meaning and oral comprehension techniques.
6. Book Talk is structured with three reasons to read, which are taken from the *Reading Rainbow*. One reason is taken from the top layer of the rainbow under FANTASTIC. The second reason is taken from the STYLISTIC layer. The third reason is taken from the ANALYTICS layer. These are introduced to the pupils in chunks and it is through these generic lenses they think and discuss their reading material.
7. The sessions work best if they operate like conversations about books and 'hands up' is not used, so there is a natural flow of talk about what they are reading.
8. During these sessions, the pleasure principle of reading is fostered and highly engaging picture books should be used in favour of phonic-based books to heighten engagement and excitement.
9. 'Book Talk' is sharply focused on reading for meaning, listening to friends read and talking about books.
10. During sessions, group members can either take turns to read, read in pairs or read to themselves. The teacher can direct this.

How 'Book Talk' is set up:

The Training Space

SATs DATA 2017

STOP PRESS 1:
33% MORE PUPILS AT EXPECTED OR ABOVE

Briary Primary School - Kent

School type: Foundation School   Age range of pupils: 4-11
Number of pupils on role: 405   Book Talk implemented: January 2017

2016 SATs Results - 42% at expected or above (7% at greater depth)
2017 SATs Results - 75% at expected or above (30% at greater depth)

"Book Talk can seriously mobilise change for the reading curriculum. If your reading provision has stagnated, then Book Talk can inject a vibrancy and support pupils to read harder texts with sharper intentions. Schools I visited deploying this approach were rich in talk and pupils read in more insightful ways."

Tammy Mitchell, Educational Consultant and Primary Improvement Adviser

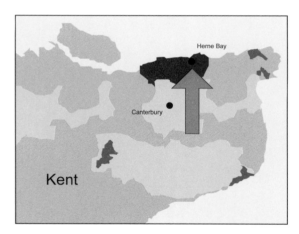

Most deprived 10% in the UK		Least deprived 10% in the UK

National average for 2017 = 71%   National average for 2016 = 66%
Source: National Curriculum Assessments at Key Stage 2 in England, 2017 (Interim)

STOP PRESS 2:
TOP PROGRESS DATA FOR A SECOND YEAR

St John's C of E Primary School - Dorking

School type: Academy Sponsor-Led   Age range of pupils: 3-11
Number of pupils on role: 221   Book Talk implemented: September 2015

2017 SATs Results
83% at expected or above
(including 17% at greater depth)

"Over the past two years, our school has fully embedded 'Book Talk' into daily practice from Reception to Year 6. As a result, progress scores were in the top 5% for reading in 2017. Our work with Jane Considine has been fundamental in our school's progress and our children's outcomes, helping the school's Ofsted rating go from Inadequate to GOOD in 3 years. Thank you!"

Mark Richards, Headteacher

	Reading	Writing	Maths
School progress score Confidence interval	**+5.79** +2.83 to +8.75	**+5.03** +2.16 to +7.91	**+7.70** +4.75 to +10.64
Well above national average About 10% of schools in England	●	●	●
Above national average About 10% of schools in England			
Average About 60% of schools in England			
Below national average About 10% of schools in England			
Well below national average About 10% of schools in England			

National average for 2017 = 71%   National average for 2016 = 66%
Source: National Curriculum Assessments at Key Stage 2 in England, 2017 (Interim)

STOP PRESS 3:
NEARLY A QUARTER ON TOP SCORES

Long Buckby Junior School - Northampton

School type: Community   Age range of pupils: 7-11
Number of pupils on role: 191   Book Talk implemented: January 2015

2017 SATs Results

☑ 77% at expected standard
☑ 13% increase from 2016
☑ 22% of pupils were high scorers (110+)
☑ 1 pupil achieved the magic 120

Internal data:

Year 3:   Sept 20% - May 66%
Year 4:   Sept 24% - May 74%
Year 5:   Sept 41% - May 91%
Year 6:   Sept 56% - May 77%

"Reading is a strength of the school and achievement has risen steadily. Pupils enjoy reading and do so for both pleasure and information. The pupils who read to the inspector were very eager to discuss their books and demonstrated good reading skills, with the most-able pupils having outstanding skills."

January 2015 OFSTED Report

National average for 2017 = 71%   National average for 2016 = 66%
Source: National Curriculum Assessments at Key Stage 2 in England, 2017 (Interim)

READING ENJOYMENT = HIGHER RESULTS

"Reading enjoyment is also connected to reading behaviour, reading motivation and reading skills. More pupils who enjoy reading read daily, more widely and more books compared to those who don't enjoy reading."

National Literacy Trust 2017 - Celebrating Reading for Enjoyment.

"Definitely pick up a book and start reading. If it's not for you, pick up another one because once you find the right book then you can't stop reading and you'll be hooked."

Sophia, Aged 11

✳ **Achieved a standardised score of 120 - May 2017** ✳

Sophia's top 3 reading list

1. **The Blood of Olympus**
Author: Rick Riordan

2. **Artemis Fowl**
Author: Eoin Colfer

3. **Subtle Knife**
Author: Philip Pullman

Children are motivated by reading both to humans and animals. These 'Reading Rabbits' love to hear new stories.

Referencing

All-Party Parliamentary Group on Literacy *Boys' Reading Commission* (2012), compiled by the National Literacy Trust.

Anglin, J. M. *Vocabulary Development: A Morphological Analysis.* Published in 1993 by Wiley on behalf of the Society for Research in Child Development.

Alvermann, D. E. *Reading adolescents' reading identities: Looking back to see ahead* (2001). Journal of Adolescent and Adult Literacy.

Baker, L. *Engaging Young Readers: Promoting Achievement and Motivation* (2000).

Barr, R. *Handbook of Reading Research, Volume III.* Publisher: Routledge (April, 2000).

Baumann, J. F. *Engaged Reading for Pleasure and Learning: A report from the National Reading Research Center, Athens, GA. (1997).*

Block, E. *The Comprehension Strategies of Second Language Readers* (1986).

Brown, A. L. *Macrorules for Summarizing Texts: The Development of Expertise* (1983). Center for the Study of Reading, University of Illinois.

Clay, M. M. *Reading Recovery: A Critical Review* (1979).

Cremin, T. *Understanding boys' (dis) engagement with reading for pleasure.* (www.researchgate.net/profile/ Teresa_Cremin/publication/315476433_ Understanding_boys'_disengagement_ with_reading_for_pleasure/ links/58d262d4458515b8d2870650/ Understanding-boys-disengagement-with- reading-for-pleasure.pdf).

Cremin, T. et al. *Building Communities of Engaged Readers: Reading for Pleasure.* Published by Routledge (2014). Cremin, T., Mottram, M., Collins, F. M., Powell, S. and Safford, K.

Dale, E. *Vocabulary measurement: techniques and major findings* (1965).

Dreher, M. J. *Engaging Young Readers: Promoting Achievement and Motivation* (2000).

Driggs, C. *Reading Reconsidered: A Practical Guide to Rigorous Literacy Instruction.* Published by Jossey-Bass (2016).

Duffy, A. M. *Engaged Reading for Pleasure and Learning: A report from the National Reading Research Center, Athens, GA. (1997).*

Ellis, S. *Phonics: Practice, Research and Policy.* Published in association with the UKLA by SAGE Publications Ltd. (2006).

Frater, G. *Observed in practice, English in the National Literacy Strategy: Some Reflections (2000).*

Gaiman, N. *Fiction has two uses...The Guardian (2013).* An abridged version of Gaiman's 2013 lecture for the Reading Agency, delivered at the Barbican in London.

Guthrie, T. J. *Engaging Young Readers: Promoting Achievement and Motivation (2000).*

Kamil, M. L. *Handbook of Reading Research, Volume III.* Publisher: Routledge (April, 2000).

Heppell, S. *Learnometer project: a suite of components to progress learning, through ICT, policy and design (with Microsoft).* **www.learnometer.net**

Institute for Fiscal Studies *English Longitudinal Study of Ageing.* Published by Oxford University Press on behalf of the International Epidemiological Association (2012).

Jackanory *a BBC children's television series designed to stimulate interest in reading, which ran from 1965 to 1996. The final story, The House at Pooh Corner by A. A. Milne, was read by Alan Bennett on 24 March, 1996. The show was briefly revived in November, 2006 for two one-off stories.*

Jenkins et al. *Literacy, Numeracy and Disadvantage Among Older Adults in England (2011).* National Research and Development Centre for Adult Literacy and Numeracy. Final report for Nuffield Foundation by: **Jenkins, A., Ackerman, R., Frumkin, L., Salter, E. and Vorhaus, J.** Institute of Education, University of London.

Juel, C. *Learning to read and write: A longitudinal study of 54 children from first through fourth grades (1988).* Department of Curriculum and Instruction, University of Texas at Austin. Journal of Educational Psychology.

Lewis, M. *Phonics: Practice, Research and Policy.* Published in association with the UKLA by SAGE Publications Ltd. (2006).

Liben, D. *Aspects of Text Complexity: Vocabulary Research Base (2010).*

Learnometer project a 10-year study by Bournemouth University (see **Heppell, S.**)

Lemov, D. *Reading Reconsidered: A Practical Guide to Rigorous Literacy Instruction.* Published by Jossey-Bass (2016).

McCandless, D. *Information is Beautiful.* First published by Collins (2009).

Medwell, J. et al. *Effective Teachers of Literacy* was commissioned by the Teacher Training Agency to boost understanding of effective teaching and how it helps children to become literate. University of Exeter (1998) **Medwell, J., Wray, D., Poulson, L. and Fox, R.**

Miller, G. A. *Vocabulary Development: A Morphological Analysis.* Published in 1993 by Wiley on behalf of the Society for Research in Child Development.

Moran, C. *"A library in the middle of a community"…* The Times Magazine (August, 2011).

Moore, D. W. et al. *Adolescent Literacy: A position statement for the Commission on Adolescent Literacy (International Reading Association).* **Moore, D. W., Bean, T. W., Birdyshaw, D., & Rycik, J. A. (1999).** Newark, DE.

Morrisroe, J. *Literacy Changes Lives 2014: A new perspective on health, employment and crime.* National Literacy Trust.

Mosenthal, P. B. *Handbook of Reading Research, Volume III.* Publisher: Routledge (April, 2000).

Murphy Paul, A. *Reading Literature Makes Us Smarter and Nicer.* Published by Time magazine, NYC (2013).

National Curriculum in England 2014: English programmes of study *"The overarching aim for English in the national curriculum is to promote high standards of language and literacy by equipping pupils with a strong command of spoken and written language, and to develop their love of literature through widespread reading for enjoyment."*

National Literacy Trust *Boys' Reading Commission (2012): The report of the All-Party Parliamentary Literacy Group Commission.*

National Reading Panel, USA *Teaching Children to Read: An Evidence-Based Assessment of the Scientific Research Literature on Reading and its Implications for Reading Instruction (2000).*

Nielsen, J. *How People Read on the Web: The Eyetracking Evidence.* NielsenNorman Group (1997).

OLASS English and Maths Assessments: Participation 2014/15 Published in 2015 by the Government's *Skills Funding Agency* (www.gov.uk/ government/statistical-data-sets/fe-data-library-education-and-training).

Organisation for Economic Cooperation & Development *PISA Reading Performance (2015).* Published in 2016 (https://data.oecd.org/pisa/reading-performance-pisa.htm).

Organisation for Economic Cooperation & Development (2010) *PISA 2009 Results: Learning to Learn – Student Engagement, Strategies and Practices (Volume III).* (http://dx.doi.org/10.1787/9789264083943-en).

Oxford English Dictionary Published by: Oxford University Press.

Paribakht, T. S. *Assessing Second Language Vocabulary Knowledge: Depth vs. Breadth.* Canadian Modern Language Review (1996).

Pearson, P. D. *Handbook of Reading Research, Volume III.* Publisher: Routledge (April, 2000).

Pinker, S. *"Children are wired for sound"…an extract from Pinker's foreword to* Why Our Children Can't Read And What We Can Do About It *by Diane McGuinness. Publisher: The Free Press, NYC (1997).*

Plato *"Every heart sings a song"…*

Programme for International Student Assessment (PISA) *see Organisation for Economic Cooperation & Development.*

Proust, M. *"There are perhaps no days of our childhood we lived so fully"… taken from Marcel Proust and John Ruskin On Reading,* edited and translated by Damion Searls, Hesperus Press Ltd. (2011).

Pullman, P. *"And we are active about the process"…*on the features that make reading pleasurable. Cited in: *Reading for Pleasure: A Research Overview* by **Clark, C.** and **Rumbold, K.** for the National Literacy Trust (2006).

Rose, J. Sir *Independent Review of the Primary Curriculum: Final Report (2009).*

Shakespeare, W. *"Words are easy"…*taken from *The Passionate Pilgrim,* first published by William Jaggard in 1599.

Sims Bishop, R. *Mirrors, Windows & Sliding Glass Doors,* taken from *Perspectives: Choosing and Using Books for the Classroom 6.3 (Summer, 1990).*

Sophocles *"One word frees us of all the weight and pain of life"….*

Wakefield, P.C. *Vocabulary Development: A Morphological Analysis.* Published in 1993 by Wiley on behalf of the Society for Research in Child Development.

Wesche, M. *Assessing Second Language Vocabulary Knowledge: Depth vs. Breadth.* Canadian Modern Language Review (1996).

Wolf, M. *Proust & The Squid: The Story and Science of the Reading Brain.* Icon Books Ltd. (2008).

Wilde, O. *"Never love anyone who treats you like you're ordinary."*

Woolway, E. *Reading Reconsidered: A Practical Guide to Rigorous Literacy Instruction.* Published by Jossey-Bass (2016).

Bibliography & Celebration of Children's Literature

Titles mentioned in this book, plus ★ Recommended reading for primary pupils

100 Hugs by Chris Riddell *(Macmillan Children's Books).*

A Child's Garden: A Story of Hope by Michael Foreman *(Walker Books).*
★ Recommended

'A library in the middle of a community…' by Caitlin Moran *(Columnist, The Times Magazine, August, 2011).*

All Join In by Quentin Blake *(Red Fox, Random House Children's Publishers).*

'And we are active about the process…' P. Pullman on the features that make reading pleasurable – cited in Reading for Pleasure: A Research Overview by C. Clark and K. Rumbold *(National Literacy Trust, 2006).*

Assessing Second Language Vocabulary Knowledge: Depth vs. Breadth by M. Wesche & T. S. Paribakht *(Canadian Modern Language Review, 1996).*

Azzi in Between by Sarah Garland *(Frances Lincoln Children's Books).*
★ Recommended

Barnaby Grimes series by Chris Riddell *(Random House Children's Publishers).*

Beast Quest series by Adam Blade *(Orchard Books).*

Bill's New Frock by Anne Fine *(Egmont Publishing).*

Black Dog by Levi Pinfold *(Templar Publishing).* ★ Recommended

Blackberry Blue and other Fairy Tales by Jamila Gavin; illustrated by Richard Collingridge *(Tamarind).*
★ Recommended

Boy In The Tower by Polly Ho-Yen *(Doubleday).*

Boys' Reading Commission (2012) from the All-Party Parliamentary Group on Literacy *(National Literacy Trust).*

Bridge to Terabithia by Katherine Paterson *(HarperCollins Publishers).*

Building Communities of Engaged Readers: Reading for Pleasure by T. Cremin et al *(Routledge, 2014).*

Carrying The Elephant: A Memoir of Love and Loss by Michael Rosen *(Penguin Books).* ★ Recommended

Cave Baby by Julia Donaldson and Emily Gravett *(Macmillan Children's Books)*. ★ Recommended

Charlie & The Chocolate Factory – Chapter 4: The Golden Tickets – by Roald Dahl *(Puffin Books)*.

'Children are wired for sound…' from S. Pinker's foreword to Why Our Children Can't Read And What We Can Do About It by D. McGuinness *(The Free Press, NYC, 1997)*.

Cloud Bursting by Malorie Blackman *(Yearling, Random House Children's Publishers)*.

Clown by Quentin Blake *(Red Fox, Random House Children's Publishers)*.
★ Recommended

Cosmic Disco by Grace Nichols; illustrated by Alice Wright *(Frances Lincoln Children's Books)*. ★ Recommended

Dare To Be Different – A Celebration of Freedom by Elana Bergin, Malorie Blackman and Fiona Waters *(Bloomsbury Publishing)*. ★ Recommended

Dirty Bertie by David Roberts & Alan MacDonald *(Little Tiger Press)*.

Double Act by Jacqueline Wilson *(Yearling, Random House Children's Publishers)*.

Dreams of Freedom – In Words and Pictures (Amnesty International) *(Frances Lincoln Children's Books)*. ★ Recommended

'Eddie' poems by Michael Rosen *(Puffin Books)*.

Enemy: A Book About Peace by Davide Cali *(Wilkins Farago)*. ★ Recommended

English Longitudinal Study of Ageing from the Institute for Fiscal Studies *(Oxford University Press, on behalf of the InternationalEpidemiologicalAssociation, 2012)*.

English programmes of study (EYFS to Year 6) '…and to develop their love of literature through widespread reading for enjoyment'. (National Curriculum in England, 2014).

Fantastic Flying Books of Mr Morris Lessmore by W. E. Joyce *(Simon & Schuster Australia)*. ★ Recommended

'Fiction has two uses…' an abridged version of N. Gaiman's 2013 lecture for the Reading Agency at the Barbican, London *(The Guardian, 2013)*.

Flat Stanley by Jeff Brown *(Egmont Publishing)*.

Flood by Alvaro F Villa *(Curious Fox)*.
★ Recommended

Flour Babies by Anne Fine *(Puffin Books)*.

For The Right To Learn – Malala Yousafzai's Story by Rebecca Langston-George *(Capstone Press)*.
★ Recommended

Girl in Tears by Jacqueline Wilson *(Corgi, Random House Children's Publishers)*.

Goggle-eyes by Anne Fine *(Puffin Books)*.

Gorilla by Anthony Browne *(Walker Books)*. ☆ Recommended

Guinness World Records 2017 *(Guinness World Records Ltd.)*.

Handbook of Reading Research, Volume III R. Barr, P. B. Mosenthal, P. D. Pearson, *(Routledge, 2000)*.

Harry Potter and the Goblet of Fire by J.K. Rowling *(Bloomsbury Publishing)*.

Here I Am by Patti Kim and Sonia Sánchez *(Curious Fox)*. ☆ Recommended

Here I Stand – Stories That Speak For Freedom (Amnesty International) *(Walker Books)*. ☆ Recommended

His Dark Materials (trilogy) by Philip Pullman *(Scholastic)*.

How People Read on the Web: The Eyetracking Evidence by J. Nielsen *(Nielsen Norman Group, 1997)*.

How to Heal a Broken Wing by Bob Graham *(Walker Books)*. ☆ Recommended

I am Malala: The Girl Who Stood Up for Education and Was Shot by the Taliban (Hardback) by Malala Yousafzai with Christina Lamb *(Orion Publishing)*. ☆ Recommended

I am not a Loser by Jim Smith *(Egmont Publishing)*.

Information is Beautiful by D. McCandless *(First published by Collins, 2009)*.

Journey by Aaron Becker *(Walker Books)*. ☆ Recommended

Kensuke's Kingdom by Michael Morpurgo *(Egmont Publishing)*.

Learning to read and write: A longitudinal study of 54 children from first through fourth grades (1988) by C. Juel *(Journal of Educational Psychology)*.

Literacy Changes Lives 2014: A new perspective on health, employment and crime by J. Morrisroe *(National Literacy Trust)*.

Lost and Found by Oliver Jeffers *(HarperCollins Children's Books)*. ☆ Recommended

Mister Magnolia by Quentin Blake *(Red Fox, Random House Children's Publishers)*.

Noughts and Crosses by Malorie Blackman *(Random House Children's Publishers)*.

OLASS English and Maths Assessments: Participation 2014/15 *(Skills Funding Agency, 2015)* www.gov.uk/government/statistical-data-sets/fe-data-library-education-and-training

On Reading M. Proust, edited and translated by Damion Searls *(Hesperus Press, 2011)*.

Once series by Morris Gleitzman *(Puffin Books)*.

One Dog & His Boy by Eva Ibbotson *(Marion Lloyd Books)*.

One World Together by Catherine and Lawrence Anholt *(Frances Lincoln Children's Books)*. ★ Recommended

Oxford English Dictionary *(Oxford University Press)*.

Phonics: Practice, Research and Policy by M. Lewis & S. Ellis *(SAGE Publications, in association with the UKLA, 2006)*.

Pig Heart Boy by Malorie Blackman *(Corgi, Random House Children's Publishers)*.

PISA 2009 Results: Learning to Learn – Student Engagement, Strategies and Practices (Volume III) Organisation for Economic Cooperation & Development (Published in 2010 - http://dx.doi. org/10.1787/9789264083943-en).

PISA Reading Performance (2015) Organisation for Economic Cooperation & Development (Published in 2016 – https://data.oecd.org/pisa/reading-performance-pisa.htm).

Private Peaceful by Michael Morpurgo *(HarperCollins Publishers)*.

Proust & The Squid: The Story and Science of the Reading Brain by M. Wolf *(Icon Books)*.

Ranger's Apprentice series by John Flanagan *(Puffin Books)*.

Reading adolescents' reading identities: Looking back to see ahead by D. E. Alvermann *(Journal of Adolescent and Adult Literacy, 2001)*.

Reading for Pleasure: A Research Overview by C. Clark and K. Rumbold *(National Literacy Trust, 2006)*.

Reading Literature Makes Us Smarter and Nicer by A. Murphy Paul *(Time magazine, NYC, 2013)*.

Reading Reconsidered: A Practical Guide to Rigorous Literacy Instruction by D. Lemov, C. Driggs & E. Woolway *(Jossey-Bass, 2016)*.

Refuge – The Timeless Story of Christmas by Anne Booth and Sam Usher *(Nosy Crow)*. ★ Recommended

Return by Aaron Becker *(Candlewick Press)*. ★ Recommended

Rooftoppers by Katherine Rundell *(Faber & Faber)*. ★ Recommended

Running on the Cracks by Julia Donaldson *(Egmont Publishing)*.

Sad Book by Michael Rosen *(Walker Books)*.

She Wore Red Trainers by Na'ima B Robert *(Kube Publishingw)*. ☆ Recommended

Something Else by Kathryn Cave and Chris Riddell *(Puffin Books)*.
☆ Recommended

The Arrival by Shaun Tan *(Hodder Children's Books)*. ☆ Recommended

The Butterfly Lion by Michael Morpurgo *(HarperCollins Publishers)*.

The Girl of Ink & Stars by Kiran Millwood Hargrave *(Chicken House)*. ☆ Recommended

The Green Ship by Quentin Blake *(Red Fox, Random House Children's Publishers)*.

The Gruffalo by Julia Donaldson *(Macmillan Children's Books)*.

The Hobbit by J. R. R. Tolkien *(HarperCollins Publishers)*.

The Huntress: Sea by Sarah Driver *(Egmont Publishing)*. ☆ Recommended

The Illustrated Mum by Jacqueline Wilson *(Yearling, Random House Children's Publishers)*.

The Island by Armin Greder *(Allen & Unwin)*. ☆ Recommended

The Journey by Francesca Sanna *(Flying Eye Books)*. ☆ Recommended

The Last Wolf by Michael Morpurgo *(Yearling, Random House Children's Publishers)*.

The Lost Thing by Shaun Tan *(Hodder Children's Books)* ☆ Recommended

The Matchbox Diary by Paul Fleischman; illustrated by Bagram Ibatoulline *(Candlewick Press)*. ☆ Recommended

The Promise by Nicola Davies; illustrated by Laura Carlin *(Walker Books)*.
☆ Recommended

The Shrinking of Treehorn by Florence Parry Heide *(Puffin Books)*.

The Step Monster by Joanna Nadin *(Egmont Publishing)*.

The Storm Whale by Benji Davies *(Simon & Shuster Children's UK)*. ☆ Recommended

The Story of Tracy Beaker by Jacqueline Wilson *(Yearling, Random House Children's Publishers)*.

The Tulip Touch by Anne Fine *(Puffin Books)*.

The Unforgotten Coat by Frank Cottrell Boyce *(Walker Books)*. ☆ Recommended

The Whale by Vita Murrow *(Templar Publishing)*. ☆ Recommended

The Wolf Wilder by Katherine Rundell *(Bloomsbury Publishing)*. ☆ Recommended

The Wreck of the Zanzibar by Michael Morpurgo *(Egmont Publishing)*.

There is a Tribe of Kids by Lane Smith *(Two Hoots; Main Market Ed).*
★ Recommended

There's a Boy in the Girls' Bathroom by Louis Sachar *(Bloomsbury Publishing).*
★ Recommended

Under the Same Sky by Britta Teckentrup *(Caterpillar Books).* ★ Recommended

Under the Weather: Stories about Climate Change edited by Tony Bradman *(Frances Lincoln Children's Books).*
★ Recommended

Vocabulary Development: A Morphological Analysis by J. M. Anglin, G. A. Miller & P. C. Wakefield *(Published by Wiley, on behalf of the Society for Research in Child Development, 1993).*

Voices in the Park by Anthony Browne *(Corgi, Random House Children's Publishers).*

We Are All Born Free – The Universal Declaration of Human Rights in Pictures (Amnesty International) *(Frances Lincoln Children's Books).* ★ Recommended

Welcome to Nowhere by Elizabeth Laird *(Macmillan Children's Books).*

We're Going On A Bear Hunt by Michael Rosen *(Walker Books).*

When Jessie Came Across The Sea by Amy Hest and P J Lynch *(Walker Books).*
★ Recommended

Who are Refugees and Migrants? What makes People Leave their Homes? And Other Big Questions by Michael Rosen and Annemarie Young *(Wayland).*
★ Recommended

Why Our Children Can't Read And What We Can Do About It by Diane McGuinness *(The Free Press, NYC, 1997).*

Window by Jeannie Baker *(Walker Books).*
★ Recommended

Wonder by R J Palacio *(Corgi, Random House Children's Publishers).*

You Can't Catch Me by Michael Rosen *(Puffin Books).*

Young Samurai series by Chris Bradford *(Puffin Books).*

Zoo by Anthony Browne *(Red Fox, Random House Children's Publishers).*

Index

 www.thetrainingspace.co.uk

 info@thetrainingspace.co.uk

 01536 410078

 JaneConsidineEducation

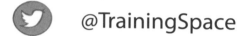 @TrainingSpace

 Thetrainingspace